Communications Research

COMMUNICATIONS RESEARCH

The Challenge of the Information Age

Edited by

NANCY WEATHERLY SHARP

SYRACUSE UNIVERSITY PRESS

Copyright © 1988 by Syracuse University Press
Syracuse, New York 13244-5160

First Published 1988

All Rights Reserved

First Edition

96 95 94 93 92 91 90 89 88   6 5 4 3 2 1

The paper used in this publication meets the minimum requirements of American National
Standard for Information Sciences—Permanence of Paper for Printed Library Materials, ANSI
Z39.48-1984. ∞™

Library of Congress Cataloging-in-Publication Data

Communications research.

    Includes index.
    1. Mass media—Research.   2. Communication—Research.
I. Sharp, Nancy Weatherly.
P91.3.C65 1988   001.51 ′ 072   88-2159
ISBN 0-8156-2432-8 (alk. paper)
ISBN 0-8156-2433-6 (pbk. : alk. paper)

Manufactured in the United States of America

Contents

Foreword

In the fall of 1985 we at the Newhouse School of Public Communications at Syracuse University began an examination of research in the communications field as part of an effort to reassess the role of the communications research center in our school. This inquiry led to even broader questions concerning the role of academic research in communications, or communication, as some prefer to call it.

We conferred with a number of leaders in our field during this investigation, people who could look at the field from a variety of professional and academic viewpoints.

One of the newspaper journalists we consulted was Norman E. Isaacs. He suggested that we hold a conference to look for the answers we were seeking. Syracuse University Chancellor Melvin A. Eggers and Vice Chancellor for Academic Affairs Gershon Vincow endorsed the project enthusiastically, and we asked Mr. Isaacs to be the conference coordinator.

As a result of Norman Isaacs' careful planning, and with funding provided by the John Ben Snow Chair in Newspaper Research and the Newhouse School, leaders from both academia and industry gathered in Syracuse in December 1985 to discuss—with great passion, as it turned out—the successes and failures of communications research and to point directions for the future. As it happened, most of the interest was in mass media research; that, then, served as the real focus for the conference.

In this book we hope to share what we learned in Syracuse with a wider audience and to go beyond the findings of the conference. The first section of the book comprises updated versions of the stimulating papers written for the gathering by three respected scholars: Everette E. Dennis, executive director of the Gannett Center for Media Studies affiliated with Columbia University; David H. Weaver, director of media research at Indiana University; and Frederick T. C. Yu, now acting dean of Columbia University's Graduate School of Journalism. They cover the past, present, and future of communications research.

The second section is a summary of the many insights, opinions, and arguments that were exchanged by the conference participants during the three days they were in Syracuse. The participants delved into the problems and burdens they saw as hampering research efforts and looked for ways of getting around them in the future.

In the third and final section we have gone beyond the conference to solicit thoughtful statements on communications research from an even wider group of people with a variety of vantage points.

Taking all three sections together we hope that our book will stand as an introduction to this crucial and exciting field for media professionals and beginning communications graduate students throughout the country and also as a signpost for future directions for communications scholars. Not only does the book acquaint readers with what has gone before in communications research and the work that is being done today, it also forecasts what the future might bring.

We at Syracuse University see this book—including, of course, the conference that brought it into being—as a significant event in the history of communications research. We were, then, especially pleased when this opinion was volunteered by our respected colleague, George Gerbner, dean of the Annenberg School of Communications at the University of Pennsylvania who also serves as editor of the influential *Journal of Communication*. His is the journal that was widely hailed for its summer 1983 issue exploring the role of communications research in society through a collection of essays by several dozen internationally prominent scholars.

"It may be that at this conference," Gerbner said while he was attending the event in Syracuse, "which is the first conference that I know of that has been assembled and has made some capital investment in the consideration of the question of where we are and where we should go from here, marks not only a milestone but a turning point in the history of our discipline. I am perfectly content to say that anything that has transpired before can be called 'Before Syracuse.'"

The Newhouse School at Syracuse University is proud to have been involved with this effort to pinpoint the current position of communications research as a scholarly undertaking and to help set its sails for the decades to come. And we hereby pledge our university and school to be at the heart of communications research "After Syracuse."

Edward C. Stephens, Dean
S. I. Newhouse School of
Public Communications
Syracuse University

Preface

The vast majority of people in Western society know about the importance of research—theoretical and applied—in health, medicine, and the broad scientific fields. What they know too little about is research in one of the most important and vital of all of society's undertakings: communications.

This is what this book is about: the extent and scope of current research activity into communications—where it has been failing and where it probably ought to be heading. It comes out of an exciting weekend conference in early December 1985—a meeting brought into being because Melvin A. Eggers, chancellor and president of Syracuse University, and Edward Stephens, dean of the S. I. Newhouse School of Public Communications, recognized a widening and dismaying gap between those in professional communications research and those involved in similar research in the universities. What made it exciting and useful was the unusual candor that marked the weekend of exchanges between those drawn from the professional and academic ranks.

The British philosopher Bertrand Russell may have explained the importance of research best when he wrote: "What we need is not the will to believe, but the wish to find out, which is the opposite."[1] It has been proved time and again that no matter what the field—government, business, industry, or anything else—the judgment of leaders and their associates is no better than their information.

There is no question that done honorably and with professional skill, the expansion of the citizens' knowledge about public affairs comes from the mass media. Not only do the mass media have the capacity to inform, they are the principal agencies in helping the public reach consensus on major social issues. The internal struggle, as it has always been, is for responsible performance. This is where the importance of research comes into consideration.

The frankness and earnestness of those who participated in the conference will become clear in the pages that follow. What struck us most forcefully was the evident desire of leading academics for far closer relationships with professionals in media practice and those engaged in research. They clearly see the need for research into the substantive issues that constantly confront citizens and their chosen political representatives.

We believe it is necessary to underline our belief in the process that was started at Syracuse. While the proposal poses funding problems, we hold that there must be a replication of such a conference—if not every year, at least every other year. We also believe there is considerable merit in the suggestion advanced by Louis D. Boccardi, president of The Associated Press, for the publication of a quarterly newsletter that would report on the best research work so that practitioners in the professional fields could relate the findings to the communications flow with more precision.

It is our conviction that only through a continuing interplay of ideas and frank exchange of opinion can there come a better understanding of the many opportunities existing for the study of important subjects, along with a stronger partnership between those directly involved in the daily flow of transmitting information and those who are tutoring students aspiring to professional careers in the various fields of public communications.

Good research on substantive matters brings knowledge—and learning how to use that knowledge brings wisdom for journalists and citizens alike.

With that realization, and recognition the unceasing pressures coming from those who would limit the free flow of information, all of us must always keep in mind a charge that has guided so many of us in our public positions. In 1644, John Milton wrote in his pamphlet, "Areopagitica:" "Though all the winds of doctrine were let loose to play upon the earth, so Truth be in the field, we do ingloriously, by licensing and prohibiting, to misdoubt her strength. Let her and Falsehood grapple: who ever knew Truth put to the worse in a free and open encounter?"

Norman E. Isaacs
Frank Stanton

Acknowledgments

This book owes much to many people. Without their contributions in terms of interest, ideas, funding support, and hard work, it would not exist.

In the early stages it was former editor and academician, Norman Isaacs, who proposed the idea of a conference to examine the problem that is at the heart of the book—the viability of communications research. Then he took the next step by organizing and coordinating the event under the leadership of Dean Edward C. Stephens of the S. I. Newhouse School of Public Communications and with the help of the school's assistant dean, Judith Van Nostrand. Funding was supplied by generous grants from both the John Ben Snow and S. I. Newhouse foundations.

During the conference, Frank Stanton, president emeritus of CBS Inc., kept the interchange of ideas moving along in his role as moderator, and Patrick J. Reagan, court reporter, created an excellent transcript of the proceedings under difficult conditions. Walda Metcalf, former editor-in-chief of the Syracuse University Press, attended some of the conference sessions and solicited the manuscript for the press. She offered valuable guidance throughout the editorial process, as did Dean Stephens.

The three scholars whose papers served as focal points for the conference —Everette E. Dennis, executive director of the Gannett Center for Media Studies; David H. Weaver, professor and director of the Bureau of Media Research at Indiana University; and Frederick T. C. Yu, acting dean of the Columbia University Graduate School of Journalism—encouraged the project and cheerfully responded to requests for help. Particular thanks go to Dennis whose suggestion was the basis for Part III.

In the preparation of Part II and in the editing of the entire manuscript I was fortunate to have knowledgeable colleagues with whom I could confer, including Samuel V. Kennedy III (who opened his voluminous files to me),

John Mitchell and Cleve Mathews. Judith VanSlyke Turk, a faculty member at the H. H. Herbert School of Journalism and Mass Communication at the University of Oklahoma; Bill Rivers, Paul C. Edwards Professor of Communication at Stanford University; and Jim Gies, assistant to Chancellor Melvin A. Eggers of Syracuse University read the manuscript and made valuable suggestions. As always, my husband, James Roger Sharp, professor of history at Syracuse University, was a great resource and support.

Other contributors to the manuscript also pointed to colleagues who had offered them special help. Professor Weaver expressed his gratitude for the suggestions of G. Cleveland Wilhoit of Indiana University. Gerald Stone asked that thanks be extended to L. Dupre Long, formerly a faculty member at Memphis State University and currently at the University of Texas at Austin. Long's respect for the English language, Professor Stone said, led to the "Eschew Obfuscation" sign he mentions in his essay.

Nancy Weatherly Sharp
Syracuse, New York
August 1, 1987

Communications Research

PART I

Communications Research
in the Past, Present, and Future

In Part I points of view on communications research are offered in three essays. Everette E. Dennis concentrates on the history of the research effort while its present is examined by David H. Weaver. Frederick T. C. Yu looks at what the future might hold.

Although each of the researchers analyzes communications research from his own particular slant on the world, the scholars share many of the same ideas and concerns so that much of what is said in the papers interconnects. Happily, as a result, each paper reinforces its companion pieces.

For instance, two of the authors discuss and evaluate the work of Paul Lazarsfeld at the Survey Research Center affiliated with Columbia University. After reading and comparing the three analyses—each representing a somewhat different point of view—the reader comes away with a richer picture of the contribution of the communications research pioneer than would have been produced by just one account.

Running through the three essays is a pervasive lack of enthusiasm over the general quality of communications research in the past and present. All three authors challenge researchers to make their work more meaningful. A major cause of the mediocrity, they note, is the fragmentation of the research effort. Scholars, they observe, too often fail to build on the work of others and this trivializes their efforts.

Whence We Came

Discovering the History of Mass Communication Research

EVERETTE E. DENNIS

C ommunication researchers almost instinctively look toward the future. As they study the impact and influence of the mass media, they are caught up in a fast-paced, continuously changing world. Whether these researchers work in industry, for media organizations, or in universities, they monitor and investigate such highly competitive and fluid phenomena as newspapers, broadcast stations, and other communication enterprises.

What is now called communication research or, often, media studies, began in the late nineteenth century with literary, legal, and historical inquiries about the press. By the 1920s sociologists had discovered this field and enriched it with institutional analyses. By the 1930s audience researchers, coming largely from the new field of broadcasting, added their imprint to the intelligence about mass communication. They did this in collaboration with leading social scientists from the universities: sociologists, psychologists, and political scientists. The field of media studies grew quickly, spurred by industrial development, wartime propaganda efforts, and the advent of high technology.

By the 1970s, communication research was a thriving enterprise that, while dominated by social scientists and their empirical methods, also engaged documentary historians and legal scholars, as well as popular culturists. While it would be difficult to argue that the field came of age then, it was at least well anchored by graduate programs, research institutes and a growing literature. Communication research even came to play a modest role in the formulation of public policy on public television, children's programming, violence, pornography, and other issues.

There was little time for reflection during the formative years. Communication research was an enterprise on the move, looking for new research questions, seeking funds, and positioning itself to address the great social questions. Occasionally, leading scholars would assay the state of communication research, but these early examinations were little more than literature reviews—syntheses of recent research with marginal connections to earlier work—most of which appeared in annual reviews of psychology, social psychology and communication.

As long as communication research remained on the periphery of such other disciplines as sociology, social psychology, and political science, scholars had no compelling reason to give much thought to its history. But, as media research developed its own niche, there came to be more reasons to wonder about its origins.

The earliest work in what can now be called "media studies" was decidedly qualitative. It was descriptive or analytical, sometimes drawing on the methods of historical research or literary criticism. It was systematic work of a humanistic sort. By the 1940s, however, quantification was in vogue and communication study emulated the world of science more than that of literature or history. To be sure, there were always historians of the press, communication law scholars and cultural essayists who did research, but the empirical scholars were in the spotlight and generally held sway. By the late 1970s this preeminence was challenged by qualitative researchers—many with an ideological bent—who decried quantification and questioned the utility and value of the prevailing research tradition. This conflict and controversy inadvertently ignited interest in the history of mass communication research.

What has resulted is a lively inquiry into the origins and growth of this important, multi-faceted field.

This contemporary preoccupation with the roots of communication research is coincident with a self-conscious assessment that asks whether we in the field know what we are talking about and whether fifty to seventy-five years of scholarship add up to anything useful or pertinent.

Knowing and understanding what mass communication can and cannot do has become a high stakes game. And, because communication research is or should be the locus for answers to compelling questions of theoretical and practical value in an age of information, the history of the field has come under the scrutiny of thoughtful people in industry and the academy. The current debate revolves around young researchers involved in cutting-edge public policy issues, audience-analysis people at the major networks, and representatives of major media research organizations who do workaday studies for newspapers, broadcast stations and cable companies. The debate that seemed to begin in the footnotes of academic journals now engages not only professors of communication but major players in the media.

A series of seminars at the Gannett Center for Media Studies at Columbia University in 1985 and 1986 provided one indication of the significance of this "history of research" debate. When organizing what we called a study group on the topic, we invited a variety of university and industry people to attend. They did and asked to bring along colleagues and students. At one meeting, vice presidents for research from three national networks attended because they thought the inquiry was important. The study group featured presentations by major figures in the field—Frank Stanton, the former CBS president and a pioneer in broadcast research; Wilbur Schramm, founder of four communication research institutes and the most widely published scholar in the field; Robert W. Merton, internationally known sociologist and a founding father of communication research; Kurt Lang, expert on the European origins of media research; James Carey, cultural critic of communication and a leader in the field; and George Gerbner, also a gifted editor and critic.

When someone asked Frank Stanton if he had been the first researcher in American broadcasting, he responded, "Oh my, no. Mal Beville was already at NBC, and there were others." Hugh M. Beville, the man mentioned, attended the next seminar. Now past 90, he had published a new book on audience research in 1984. Faculty members from Columbia and nearby schools attended regularly. Others commuted from Philadelphia, Washington, and the Midwest. By their presence they were saying, "This is important and worth my time."

The yield of the Columbia seminar was several major papers and hours of lively dialogue wherein the beginnings of communication research were debated and discussed. Who were the founders? What were their intentions? Why did they pursue particular questions? Who paid for the research and why? These and other questions inevitably came back to a seminal concern: What do we know about mass communication and the mass media?

The Gannett-Columbia study group was concurrent with interest elsewhere in the country in the history of communication research and what has been referred to as the "rewriting" of that remembered history.

Writing or "Rewriting" the History

To speak of "rewriting" the history of communication research suggests that there is an orthodoxy codified and readily available. That is not the case. When scholars refer to the "historiography" of the field or its "received history," they are describing fragments of a complex mosaic about which there is little real agreement. That disagreement centers on when and where communication research originated, who among its founders were most influential, and other questions.

Although there is no written history as such, periodic summaries of findings and trends, as well as synthesis reports, are often referred to as the "received history." Still, there is a controversy that pits researchers with one view of the past against those seeking new interpretations.

Influence of Thomas Kuhn

In a number of disciplines now reflecting on their pasts, whether glorious or not, the culprit who stimulated the critiques is a most unlikely figure—a thoughtful and measured historian of science named Thomas Kuhn. His seminal book, *The Structure of Scientific Revolutions*, published in 1962 by the University of Chicago Press, seemingly more than any other single source has fostered debate about the evolution and development of knowledge. The field of mass communication is no exception. Scholars considering the emergence of scientific knowledge about communication find concepts of change advanced by Kuhn—change by exception, incremental change, pendulum change, and paradigm collapse—a compelling framework for analysis.

Paradigm change involves a major reassessment of the way researchers have structured and, thus, have understood knowledge. That concept was on sociologist Todd Gitlin's mind in 1978 when he wrote a blistering critique of the "dominant paradigm" of mass communicatrion research.[1] He attacked the quantitative traditions of the master surveyor, Paul Lazarsfeld, and work initiated in Columbia University's Bureau of Applied Social Research. He saw Lazarsfeld and others who studied media effects with empirical methods as mere "administrative researchers" who were servants of industry bound up by "intellectual, ideological and institutional commitments"[2]

The resulting controversy has centered on the "relative importance" of the mass media in comparison with other social institutions and influences on people's attitudes and behavior. The so-called minimal effects theory of media impact and influence identified with Lazarsfeld irked Gitlin, who wrote scathingly:

> By its methodology, media sociology [mass communication research] has highlighted the recalcitrance of audiences, their resistance to media-generated messages, and not their dependency, their acquiescence, their gullibility. It has looked to "effects" of broadcast programming in specifically behaviorist fashion, defining "effects" so narrowly, microscopically, and directly as to make it very likely that survey studies could only show slight "effects" at most. It has enshrined these short run effects as "measures" of "importance" largely because these "effects" are measurable in a strict, replicable, behavioral sense, thereby deflecting attention of larger social meanings of mass media production.[3]

A number of commentators fired return salvos for, after all, the paradigm collapse critique not only challenged much of modern academic research but also such durable industry research as broadcast ratings and newspaper readership studies. Thus, commercial researchers quickly joined in the reassessment of appropriate ways to measure attitudes and opinions to determine whether media messages could bring cognitive, attitudinal, and behavioral changes.

Quite naturally, this fostered historically oriented defenses by those in the "minimal effects" tradition. It was not unusual in the late 1970s to see leading television researchers, for example, rise at scholarly meetings to defend the underlying assumptions of their work (and that of their mentors—especially Lazarsfeld). This reinforced research aimed at cognitive considerations that used such labels as "agenda-setting," "coorientation," "uses and gratifications," and others, as Donald Lewis Shaw and Maxwell McCombs have written.[4]

Progression of Interpretations

Not all of the efforts to sort out the historical development of mass communication have been associated with critiques of the so-called "dominant paradigm" of minimal effects. Some commentary has been much more matter-of-fact, even benign. Several books have attempted to organize systematic evidence about the field of mass communication along the lines of media power.[5] The thesis advanced in these books is that there has been a progression of interpretations, generally described as the *powerful, minimal,* and *return to powerful effects* schools of thought.

In this understanding of the field, early studies based mostly on impressionistic and anecdotal analysis prior to the late 1930s reinforced the notion of a powerful press, which used a "hypodermic needle" metaphor, suggesting that the media injected information into an impressionable public. With more systematic and careful measures in the 1940s (courtesy of social science), the media seemed less powerful, and thus the term "minimal effects" was coined. In the 1960s and 1970s several researchers challenged the old order and called for a reassessment of the dominant view. The German researcher Elisabeth Noelle-Neumann spoke of "the return of a concept of powerful media effects,"[6] an idea seconded by other researchers,[7] fostering what has been called the "big effects-little effects" debate. Although it is somewhat simplistic to characterize complex research patterns and trends with post-hoc buzz words not used by the original researchers, that is what has happened. Thus, the early period of communication research history is characterized by the "hypodermic needle" or big effects theory. It is, in this interpretation, replaced by the "two-step flow" paradigm of Elihu Katz and Paul Lazarsfeld. Anthony Smith notes that "as quickly as one kind of influence is denied, another springs into parlance."[8] There is an apparent need to label and characterize—sometimes even to cari-cature—research themes and trends.

The return of "big effects" was influenced by such developments as the writings of Marshall McLuhan (suggesting television was central and pervasive), the cognitive research of Shaw and McCombs, as well as British and French scholarship on the content of media (e.g., television as a text) that led to cul-tural and critical studies.

Interdisciplinary Perspectives

The writings of Wilbur Schramm and Melvin De Fleur have long pro-vided a historical explanation of mass communication research with material that blends (a) intellectual influences from various fields that have had pro-found impacts on communication research (*e.g.*, learning theory) with (b) ef-forts by social scientists who have "tarried awhile," to use Bernard Berelson's phrase, on communication problems, and (c) the work of researchers who have made this study their exclusive scholarly preoccupation.[9]

Historiography

Interest in the historiography of mass communication research is seen in articles by David Weaver and Richard Gray codifying the history of commu-nication research from a journalism school perspective; Steven H. Chaffee, from a political communication view; and Byron Reeves and Ellen Wartella, as the history of effects research concerns children. James Carey has written about the cultural underpinnings of communication research, well outside the empirical tradition, and has critiqued historical research. Gertrude Robinson offers a technological explanation in a recent critique of the history of North American communication research.[10]

There has not been much effort to trace early intellectual origins or to assess and evaluate the influences of Lord Bryce, the English traveler and ob-server who toured the United States in the late nineteenth century, or phi-losopher Walter Lippmann in a historical analysis of public opinion research. Exceptions to this are writings by Kurt Lang on the European origins of mass communication and Hanno Hardt on the German roots of social theory.[11] Most contemporary historical reviews begin in the 1940s and rarely stretch back beyond the sociological and social-psychological roots of the field. Indeed, with few exceptions, the historical, legal and literary work of scholars concerned about the media or freedom of expression gets little attention in current critiques, yet this work predated empirical efforts and has considerable continuity, having moved through several stages of development.[12]

Concurrent Streams

Neither has much been written about the concurrent streams idea that we explored at Columbia in the study group. In this historical analysis, there are several concurrent streams of activity, some of them interrelated, some not. This analysis recognizes the longstanding interchange between the academy and the communications industries. What will probably always be lacking in any historical review, though, is an insider's analysis of commercial and proprietary research. Although done to assist a particular media organization at a given time, its cumulative impact is considerable, yet rarely shared outside industry circles.

The concurrent streams analysis looks at schools of thought that have influenced and guided communication research. Because communication research emerged concurrently in interrelated fashion at various universities and in governmental and industry settings, it is useful to talk about streams of activity while still recognizing that this is a simplification of something more complex. We are discussing the European origins of mass communication research, the Columbia and Chicago "schools," the rise of mass communication research in journalism schools, the war research, industry research, and the current reassessment that features several alternative viewpoints.

The Columbia School. The Columbia School includes the work of a generation of empirical researchers who have been concerned with attitude formation, as well as tools and theories of measurement and analysis.[13] Embracing work by scholars at several universities—including Yale and Princeton—it has involved mass communication studies aimed mainly at determining the impact and effect of media messages on individuals, which, in turn, has led to the development of various theories about society and culture.

This research, largely carried out with industry and government contracts, has been eminently practical and may have influenced much of modern media marketing research. It played a major role in providing intelligence about audiences to the new and emerging radio and television industries from the 1930s through the 1950s and beyond. Preeminent in the communication capital of the country, Columbia-trained people (here I mean also those associated with the other institutions influenced by Lazarsfeld and other leading figures of the period) have taken important research jobs at the television networks and other media research organizations.

The Chicago School. Even before the Bureau of Applied Research was active at Columbia, sociologists at the University of Chicago were studying mass communication issues and problems. Under the guidance of Robert Park and others, studies at Chicago focused on problems related to the sociology of work and knowledge as well as organizational theory. This has included studies of media organizations, the nature of news, and people who work in media. Unlike the Lazarsfeld-Columbia group, the Chicago scholars have been more likely to use participant-observer methods or content analysis than survey research. At Chicago and among those influenced by its intellectual traditions, the emphasis of research has tended to be on the internal dynamics—the economics and structure of the media, the "product" of communication, and the people involved in the process.[14]

The Communication Schools. Although research was being done in journalism schools prior to the development of formal research bureaus, such activity got an infusion of energy with the establishment of institutes or centers for communication research at Stanford University and the universities of Illinois, Wisconsin, and Minnesota in the 1940s and 1950s. These programs, under the direction of such leaders as Wilbur Schramm, Ralph Casey, and Ralph Nafziger, were lively foci for projects involving contract work for industry, but they also engaged in theory construction and methodological testing. Strongly guided by the Lazarsfeld tradition and tied to public opinion research, these programs also embraced part of the Chicago tradition since they studied media organizations and their problems. Several of the principals of the new centers assisted with war research and other policy-oriented efforts after World War II. These programs trained generations of graduate students who now staff many of the nation's schools of journalism and mass communication. Some are also in industry.

The War Research. Concurrent with the Bureau of Applied Social Research and its progeny—indeed involving some of them—was government research on propaganda conducted during World War II. People from industry and the academy were employed by the government to assist with information campaigns to test various communication styles and strategies. The assumptions of those researchers were vastly different than the ones of those who had done propaganda analysis in the 1930s and before. Much of the early work belonged to the "powerful press" school, which made many conclusions about media and power without much empirical testing or analysis. The "war research" activity was continued, in concept at least, through the 1960s and 1970s in the form of governmental commissions and other efforts to examine public problems (race relations, pornography, the effects of television, etc.). This was administrative research conducted either by government agencies or by universities under contract to solve particular policy problems.[15]

Industry Research. Yet another element in the history of communication research is industry activity, which is often concerned with audiences and advertising. Much of this is medium-specific. Early efforts by Lazarsfeld and Stanton were used to scope out and grapple with the radio audience. Later this activity inspired a modern system of broadcast audience ratings. Efforts by Chilton Bush and others did the same for newspapers and their readership problems.

Organizations like the Magazine Publishers Association, the Newspaper Advertising Bureau, and the Television Advertising Bureau evolved and engaged in research aimed at proving that their medium was *best* for delivering a particular audience. The purpose was unabashedly self-serving—to help a particular medium (or media organization) ascertain its strengths and weaknesses with the audience in order to capture a large share and, thus, get more advertising revenue.

An ultimate outgrowth of this approach was the massive Newspaper Readership Project of the 1970s, which attempted to provide audience and potential audience data to arrest declining newspaper circulation. This study, perhaps more dramatically than any in recent history, led to the remodeling of many newspapers and to what has been called a "marketing approach" to news. Long before this, television audience research—some of it carried out by "media consultants"—had reshaped television entertainment and news programs.[16]

While these industry research efforts have reinforced traditional approaches, commercial studies have not been without critics. One critique of modern audience research was expressed at a 1984 conference at Columbia University titled, "Beyond Ratings," which not surprisingly contained many of the same issues one finds in attacks on the Lazarsfeld tradition.

Evaluating the Yield of Research. Today each of the concurrent streams is being analyzed and reviewed by scholars interested in the origins of communication research. Some commentators are social scientists who want to know whether understanding past research endeavors provides clues about appropriate approaches to such studies today. Others are critical theorists applying a Marxist or neo-Marxist analysis to questions about who pays for research and why.

But, to date, only a few of these historical tracings have concerned themselves in any complete way with the intellectual "bottom line." What do we really know? In what areas has the yield of research been productive and powerful and in what areas is there a paucity of evidence?

Ironically, one of the most critical examinations of the dearth of unifying theories growing out of mass communication research came not from the "young Turks" of the field but from Schramm, who asked whether the field had "produced a central interrelated body of theory on which the practitioners of a discipline can build and unify their thinking." His answer: "I am afraid that it has not."[17] The article appeared in an extraordinary issue of the *Journal of Communication* (Summer 1983) called "Ferment in the Field," which is by far the most comprehensive analysis of the current state of mass communication research.

Field or Discipline?

There are a number of ways to sort out the meaning and yield of mass communication research, but they are often encumbered by debate over whether mass communication study is a *field* or a *discipline*. Some who argue that it is a discipline look at the process and effects of communication and begin with such basic building blocks as signals, messages, and other aspects of theoretical analysis. They say that the advancement of knowledge about mass communication has now reached disciplinary status with some accepted theories and generally agreed upon assumptions. They also point to a massive literature developed by people who call themselves mass communication researchers. One proponent of this view is George Gerbner, who writes, "What makes communication a discipline is that it has something to say about every human and social situation. As do history, economics, physics or any of the established disciplines, communication has a unique contribution to make to the understanding of any human relationship or situation."[18]

Not everyone agrees with this approach. Some who believe that mass communication is a field of study rather than a discipline, for example, compare it to international communication. It is, they say, a field or topic that can and does benefit from the work of many scholars representing a wide variety of disciplines, from political science and history to psychology, sociology, economics, American studies, and law.

The distinction between discipline and field is that in the former, mass communication is preeminent as a topic for study; in the latter, it is a subset of a scholar's primary discipline, whether politics, law, or social relations. Either approach can be effective in organizing the history of the field.

Retrospectives

There is little historical material on the evolution of mass communication as a distinct discipline, tracing the contribution of other academic disciplines or fields. Neither is there a cogent history from the point of view of any of the contributing disciplines that have brought their theories and methods to bear on media or communication problems. What we do have are annual reviews of psychology, social psychology, and other disciplines that regularly inventory the present state of knowledge about mass communication from their points of view. One of the best on mass communication deals with media effects. Written by Donald F. Roberts and Christine M. Bachen, it appears in the *Annual Review of Psychology* (1981) and is part of a long line of such reviews.[19]

Various yearbooks and journals collect exemplary research done during the previous year and occasionally attempt to determine the scope of the history and direction of the field. Individual subfields, such as communication history or international communication, also occasionally evaluate their present statuses with historical analyses. For example, communication law scholars have begun to critique their past as a rationale for new methods and, thus, a new perspective on old but still important problems.[20] These and other subfield retrospectives usually have as their purpose a "past is prologue" analysis. The contours and currents of the field are examined for their pertinence to the contemporary scene. Indeed, their authors rarely think of these reports as history.

Answering Society's Questions

A truly telling review of the history of mass communication research would ask whether the major questions of society had been addressed. A cursory review might be a useful indicator of the true status of mass communication research, not just its historical contours, but the nature, dimensions, scope, and quality of its contributions.

What have mass communication researchers studied? In addition to the categories of research mentioned in annual reviews, the field has often been divided into three parts: *external* research (effects and other media-society issues); *internal* research (the inner workings of communication organizations); and media *criticism and analysis* of both.

A large and perhaps overarching concern has been media power—the impact, influence, and effect of mass communication. Scholars have not always shared common definitions or engaged in precisely comparable studies, but this has been a consistent theme in media research, and no other topic has approached it as a dominant concern. Most of the work has been empirical, has used systematic methods, and typically (but not always) has employed quantitative measures. There also has been a cultural and humanistic stream of effects research in studies of popular and mass culture. This largely literary tradition has been concerned with themes and patterns of media content or with the image of particular groups, individuals, or movements.

If the "media power" research has been largely external—concerned with the effects of media messages on individuals (or on society and culture) in an outward fashion—there has been another approach to research that has been more internally oriented. Sometimes called "media sociology," it most likely derived from the "Chicago School." This approach looks at the product of mass communication (news or entertainment, styles and standards of journalism, etc.); the nature of the organization (groups versus independents, management styles and approaches); media people (who they are, what they think and do, what their ethics are); and other activities within organized mass communication.

Neither internal nor external research has to be self-possessed or parochial. For example, contextual comparisons of media industries with other industries are illuminating and useful. And certainly, no effects or impact research has any real meaning without the context of other influences on the individual, groups (family, school, or religion), or society itself.

A less well developed line of communication research might simply be called media criticism and analysis. Here the tools of the historian, the literary critic, and the legal scholar are useful in probing concepts (such as the public interest or the theory of representation), themes in media criticism, and other concerns. This research is typically more normative, more concerned with the exploration of problems and solutions. Most empirical research also is problem oriented, but actually finding a solution usually is not its main aim.

In recent years, the criticism and analysis of mass communication has been augmented by the work of cultural and critical theorists (many from Britain and Europe), who have not accepted the underlying assumptions of earlier work. For example, Jay Jensen's assertion that media criticism must begin with the clear recognition of the profit orientation of the media[21] has been disputed by current critics who have challenged the existing economic order.[22]

What Graduate Programs Tell Us

In many academic disciplines, the structure of graduate programs reflects the way knowledge is organized in the field. Typically, this is not a conceptually neat, well-ordered framework. Instead, it reflects years of turf battles by faculty members. This is also true in mass communication. In a number of leading doctoral programs, research activity is organized in a fashion that separates *substantive* topics (what is studied) from *theory and methodology* (the tools for study) in such a way that the results are somewhat confusing. For example, several programs follow the model of the University of Minnesota, which divides mass communication into four subfields—theory and methodology, history of mass communication, mass communication agencies as social institutions (media sociology and law), and international mass communication. Some of these subfields emphasize substantive topics or problems; others are process- or method-oriented. This is not an anomaly at Minnesota but reflects other programs and, to some extent, the organization of the field.

Each of the subfields gives scholars "diplomatic relations" with their counterparts elsewhere. Indeed, there are "social institutions" scholars, communication historians, legal scholars, and communication theorists. A related approach is used by the Annenberg School at the University of Pennsylvania, which has a tripartite division of the field including: (1) codes and modes (the transmission of messages through various media), (2) communication behavior, and (3) communication systems and institutions. There are other formulations in other graduate programs, all reflecting a given institution's view of the field, local traditions, sources of funding, and specific interests of individual faculty members or students.

Although it can be argued that the conceptual framework of many communication graduate programs does not achieve intellectual perfection, there is an emphasis on unified areas of knowledge that cut across all forms of communication and mass communication rather than aim narrowly at a single industry and its interests. This is both a virtue and a vice. Over the long haul, the benefits of broadly-gauged study that is generalizable from one setting to another is obvious, but in the short run—and through much of the history of mass communication research—the lack of an industry orientation by many communication schools has led media professionals to think that communication research is not pertinent to their problems. Thus, industry representatives sometimes have urged scholars to organize their programs to serve particular needs, differentiating newspaper interests from those of broadcasting or advertising or cable television. Indeed, at several universities, chairs have been established that specifically target the research needs of a given industry.

While universities welcome this kind of support and it gives them useful links with industry, such medium-specific research can encourage fragmentation in understanding the larger processes of communication. At a time when all forms of communication are coming together in an electronically-based and computer-driven system, the commonality can be lost in research programs that are organized from a newspaper, magazine, or advertising point of view. The same can be said for research that is funded by business, the health care industry, or other special interests. Business and law schools have generally managed to avoid the trap inherent in research that has as its starting point a narrow interest rather than unifying concepts. Moreover, it can be argued that such an orientation duplicates the work of media industry researchers.

Universities ought to have a different role and function. A university's ability to move beyond parochial interests is important in establishing a genuine discipline that pursues knowledge rather than specific short-term goals that make headlines in the trade press. Although this may not be responsive to the "quick fix" demands of industry, it may be more useful to industry over time because of the research and development implications that are found in theory construction and in the application of new methods of analysis.

Does Research Have Any Value?

Looking at organizational patterns of communication scholarship is useful in seeing where researchers have been. It also helps focus a vital concern: Have these researchers addressed the major questions of importance to the public in general and to those who specifically care about mass communication in America? Have the great and enduring issues been considered? And, if so, with what success? Is the research worth the effort or is it a kind of "brain bank," employing talented people who are working on irrelevant matters?

Because the history has not been written in any definitive way, there are no easy answers. What one needs is not a simplistic "bottom line" accounting but instead a conceptual map that might consume many volumes and require complex presentation. In addition, there is a need for a mapping device that helps both scholars and professionals understand the contradictions and complexities of research. Still, it is useful to hazard a look at key questions, relating them to research evidence in a spirit of hypotheses-building rather than dogmatic evaluation. Since the preeminent question—that of effects, importance, and power—has already been reviewed in this discussion, I will consider other vital matters.

On questions of freedom of expression our research literature is quite thin. There are hundreds of fragmented studies of given legal cases and concepts— many fewer on freedom of expression itself. There is little that illuminates and makes sense of competing interests and rights that come into conflict with the free flow of information. What work we do have comes mainly from the field of law and legal philosophy.

On economic questions, such as those relating to the nature and meaning of ownership patterns of the media, the role of advertising, and audience analysis, again there is a very limited literature. The entire literature of the economics of mass communication is quite small, and, even though there is much current interest in media management, the field of media economics has barely emerged.

On technological questions there has been, with a few exceptions (including a study of the role of the telegraph),[23] little work on the emergence of the Information Society and on the Communication Revolution. While it is incontrovertible that books and articles on subjects like cable television, direct broadcast satellites, and videotex have a limited shelf life, it is disturbing that there is so little research being generated by mass communication researchers and others with a communication orientation. There is, of course, a good deal of technological research being carried on by engineers and lawyers, but the communication field is hardly holding its own, even on questions bearing directly on media organizations and products.[24]

On philosophical questions there is cause for some, although not a great deal of, celebration. For more than ten years, the ethics of mass communication has been a topic of central concern. There have been a number of important books and articles on media ethics. In addition, several philosophically-oriented studies of other underpinnings of mass communication have appeared. Indeed, some philosophers in mainstream philosophy departments have turned their attention to mass communication questions.[25]

What these four foregoing summaries suggest is a need for a regular, systematic inventory of what we know and what we need to know. Such an effort would encourage scholars, industry leaders, and funding sources to put efforts where the intellectual and social pay-offs could be great.

Clients and Constituents

A review of mass communication research history gives clues about the producers of such research, whether in the academic or commercial worlds, and the motivation behind their work. Some are theory-builders or scholars more interested in the tools and measurements of research, while others are responding to substantive questions important to educators, the media industries, or the public. There has been relatively little discussion of the constituency and clientele for communication research, which is also central to understanding its history.

Who are the constituents for research and how have they influenced the shape of its history? Within the university, the researchers themselves and their colleagues in journalism and communication schools are primary constituents. They have done research because they have intellectual interests in the problems to be studied and because they seek promotion and tenure in increasingly research-oriented universities. Colleagues who are not research-oriented can be secondary users of research although sometimes they are antagonists to it. Other faculty members in the university, in far-flung fields, are indirect constituents since the research enterprise of communication and journalism schools helps bring academic legitimacy. Without a perceived contribution to knowledge in a research university, faculty members and their departments suffer greatly. Students ought to be a constituency as well. They should benefit from research in their courses and contribute to it both as research assistants and as subjects of studies.

The external constituencies for communication research include media industries, government agencies, foundations, and various private organizations interested in knowing more about the media for their own priorities. They sometimes purchase, commission, and/or fund research. In recent years the output of the journalism and communication schools in meeting the needs of these various organizations has seemed modest. There is considerable criticism among media industries about the lack of pertinence of communication research in the universities, and funding agencies have not been overly generous in supporting projects in journalism and communication schools. Similarly, government agencies, which were frequently tapped for funds in the 1960s, no longer provide much support for mass communication efforts. Perhaps this is part of a decline of support for social research although funding for various technological projects is occurring in other fields.

Summary and Conclusions

This paper, which is intended to stimulate thought rather than answer questions, is written at a time when there is much interest in the history of mass communication research. The research archives have not heretofore been well-tended and, consequently, retrieving the history is an unfinished chore. What can be done is to sort out the patterns of activity, the schools of thought, and the pervasive interests of researchers. When that is done, it is clear that there will be a field (or discipline, take your pick) with a substantial corpus.

While there is communication research of the highest intellectual quality —the field has attracted giants—it is also true that the overall quality is not impressive and that much research is not especially rigorous. Thus, symposia of the kind organized by Syracuse University have enormous value in moving the research enterprise ahead. It can and ought to be improved and upgraded. It should get more support both in the academy and in industry, not for narrow or self-serving reasons but because this is an Information Age when the citizens' needs for understanding are high. The advancement of knowledge will help them and, in turn, society.

Notes

1. Todd Gitlin, "Media Sociology and the Dominant Paradigm," *Theory and Society* 6, (November 1978): 205–53.

2. Ibid., 205.

3. Ibid., 203–6.

4. Donald L. Shaw and Maxwell McCombs, *The Emergence of American Political Issues: The Agenda-Setting Function of the Press* (St. Paul, Minn.: West Publishing Co., 1977).

5. See Sydney Kraus and Dennis Davis, *The Effects of Mass Communication on Political Behavior* (University Park, Pa.: Pennsylvania State University Press, 1976); and the chapter entitled, "Power of the Press," in Everette E. Dennis and John C. Merrill, *Basic Issues in Mass Communication: A Debate* (New York: Macmillan Publishing Co., 1984).

6. Elisabeth Noelle-Neumann, "Return to the Concept of Powerful Mass Media," *Studies of Broadcasting* (1973): 67–112.

7. John P. Robinson, "Perceived Media Bias and the 1968 Vote: Can the Media Affect Behavior After All?," *Journalism Quarterly* 6 (Summer 1972): 239–45; and James Lemert, *Does Mass Communication Change Public Opinion After All?* (Chicago: Nelson-Hall, 1981).

8. Anthony Smith, "The Influence of Television" in "The Moving Image," *Daedalus* 14 (Fall 1985): 3.

9. Wilbur Schramm and William Porter, *Men, Women, Messages, and Media* (New York: Harper & Row, 1982); Melvin L. De Fleur and Sandra Ball-Rokeach, *Theories of Mass Communication*, 4th ed. (New York: Longman, 1982); and Shearon Lowery and Melvin L. De Fleur, *Milestones in Mass Communication Research* (New York: Longman, 1983).

10. David H. Weaver and Richard G. Gray, "Journalism and Mass Communication Research in the United States" in G. Cleveland Wilhoit and Harold de Bock, eds., *Mass Communication Review Yearbook*, vol. 1 (Beverly Hills, Calif.: Sage Publications, 1980), 124–51; Steven H. Chaffee, ed., *Political Communication* (Beverly Hills, Calif.: Sage Publications, 1975); Byron Reeves and Ellen Wartella, "Recurring Issues in Research on Children and Media," *Educational Technology* 23 (June 1983): 5–9; James W. Carey, "Communication and Culture," *Communication Research* 2 (Summer 1975), 173–91; and Gertrude J. Robinson, "Mass Communication in Ferment: Open Questions in the Historiography of the Field," a paper presented at the August 1985 convention of the Association for Education in Journalism and Mass Communication, Memphis, Tenn.

11. Kurt Lang, "Critical Functions of Empirical Communication Research: Observations on German-American Influences, Media," *Culture and Society* 1 (January 1979): 83–96; Hanno Hardt, *Social Theories of the Press: Early German and American Perspectives* (Beverly Hills, Calif.: Sage Publications, 1979).

12. See Weaver and Gray, "Journalism and Mass Communication Research," and Ever-

ette E. Dennis, *The Media Society, Evidence About Mass Communication in America* (Dubuque, Iowa: William C. Brown Co., 1978).

13. Allen H. Barton, "Paul Lazarsfeld and the Invention of the University Institute for Applied Social Research" in Burkhart Holzner and Jiri Nehnevajsa, eds., *Organizing for Social Research* (Cambridge, Mass.: Schenkman Publishing Co., 1982).

14. Dennis, *The Media Society*, passim.

15. Ibid., 21–33.

16. See Ron Powers, *The Newscasters* (New York: St. Martin's Press, 1977).

17. Wilbur Schramm, "The Unique Perspective of Communication: A Retrospective View," *Journal of Communication* 33 (Summer 1983): 6–17.

18. George Gerbner, "Defining the Field of Communication," *ACA Bulletin* (April 1984). The *ACA Bulletin* is published by the Association of Communication Educators.

19. Donald F. Roberts and Christine M. Bachen, "Mass Communication Effects," *Annual Review of Psychology* 32 (February 1981): 307–56.

20. Donald M. Gillmor and Everette E. Dennis, "Legal Research and Judicial Communication" in Steven H. Chaffee, ed., *Political Communication: Issues and Strategies for Research* (Beverly Hills, Calif.: Sage Publications, 1975); and Everette E. Dennis, "Frontiers in Communication Law Research," *Communications and the Law* 4 (August 1986), 3–10.

21. Jay Jensen, "A Method and Perspective for Criticism of the Mass Media," *Journalism Quarterly* 36 (Spring 1960): 262.

22. Dallas Smythe and Tran Van Dihn, "On Critical and Administrative Research: A New Critical Analysis," *Journal of Communication* 33 (Summer 1983): 117–27.

23. James Carey, "Technology and Ideology: The Case of the Telegraph," *Prospects* 13 (1983).

24. Frederick Williams, *The Communications Revolution* (Beverly Hills, Calif.: Sage Publications, 1982); and Ithiel de Sola Pool, *Technologies of Freedom* (Cambridge, Mass.: Belknap Press, 1983).

25. Among philosophy and ethics scholars who have studied media questions are Thomas Scanlon of Princeton University, Robert Meister of the University of California at Santa Cruz, and Louis Hodges of Washington and Lee University.

Mass Communication Research Problems and Promises

David H. Weaver

The history of much mass communication research in the United States is anchored in a concern with the potential harmful influences of various media and in the need to measure the audiences and uses of media for advertisers.[1] In other words, many of the milestones in U.S. mass communication research—be they academic or industry-based—are problem-oriented although it is fair to say that the academicians have been more concerned with the *effects* of various media and that those in the media industries have concentrated more on the *uses* of these media, especially on the numbers and kinds of people using specific media and specific content of these media.[2]

Regardless of emphasis on effects or uses, both academic and industry researchers generally have been more concerned with the media's *audiences* and *messages* than with the *producers* of those messages—reporters, editors, news directors, correspondents, and others who create the words and pictures that flow from newspapers, television sets, magazines, and radios. Partly because of this emphasis on audiences, and also because many researchers aren't very effective communicators, much of the research has had limited value for those of us who educate students to be better journalists and for those who work as journalists in the various media.

The late Richard Gray and I discussed this in the following passage from our brief overview of mass communication research in the United States.

> As a result of their interests in messages and effects, many mass communication researchers [have become] more concerned with audiences and the effect of journalistic messages upon them, than with journalists and the actual production of these messages. Yet during this same time, journalism educators concentrated on courses of instruction in writing, reporting, editing, history, law and ethics with the aim of training students to be better observ-

ers and message producers. Although the programs of research on media uses and effects had some relevance to these courses, it was limited. And to the working journalist, this research often seemed to have no practical value whatever, in part because few effects researchers bothered to expound on the implications of their studies for journalists, and also because many such researchers wrote the results of their studies in barely comprehensible language.[3]

This is not to say that media uses and effects research has no value for journalism educators or for working journalists. On the contrary, most journalists should have a better understanding of who their audiences are and what the effects of their messages are. But preoccupation with message and audience research has led to little interest in journalists and journalism on the part of some researchers and to only sporadic study of journalistic training and values and their effect on what is reported as news.

Of course, concern with audiences is not the only problem with much mass communication research from the viewpoint of many journalism educators and practitioners. Many journalists charge that such research is too theoretical, too abstract, too quantitative, and not written in easily understandable language. On the other side, many researchers lament the lack of theoretical development in mass communication research, the use of crude measures, and the reliance on statistical methods that are not terribly sophisticated. Some of this argument over methods is reminiscent of the old "green eyeshade—chi-square" debate in which journalists (supposedly wearing green eyeshades) were fond of quoting passages from the methods sections of *Journalism Quarterly* articles that seemed to make no sense to any reasonably intelligent user of the English language. The chi-squares (those involved in quantitative analysis), on the other hand, were equally disdainful of the journalists (and some journalism educators) who had no training in quantitative research methods.

This disagreement is a pseudo-debate that does little to illuminate the fundamental problems of mass communication research. Quantitative methods are often essential in making sense of large and complicated sets of findings, just as qualitative methods, such as in-depth interviews and direct observation, are needed for answering other questions. It is no more reasonable to expect those not trained in quantitative methods to be able to understand complicated methodology descriptions and data tables than it is for someone not trained in electronics to understand diagrams of electrical circuits.

Likewise, the frequently heard complaint from journalists and some educators that mass communication research is too theoretical and not practical enough also misses the point.[4] All of us need theories whether we practice or teach journalism. We need general guidelines or rules for allocating scarce time or space to certain kinds of news, for defining markets, for setting advertising rates and subscription prices, for dealing with problems of credibility, for thinking about the effects of what we do, and for thinking about our proper roles in society. As has been said before, there is nothing so practical as a good theory—a theory that accurately explains and predicts. The disagreement between academics and practitioners is really not over the need for theory but rather over the need for particular *kinds* of theory to address particular kinds of questions and problems.

The fundamental problems, then, are mainly problems of substance (or, more precisely, lack of it) than problems with methods. Unless interesting and important questions are asked, no study's findings will be seen as significant—especially not by those outside the community of researchers—regardless of the levels of sophistication in methods or the statistical significance of the findings. Perhaps examples of problems and promises will help.

Problems

A lack of application to important social and scholarly issues. In 1973 Peter Clarke criticized what he perceived as "trivial data" on communication and suggested that we might make "more profound contributions to human understanding if we paused now and then to ask whether the results of a proposed inquiry—any of its results—would make a difference if known."[5]

Today, there are still numerous examples of trivial research, including a recent study on portrayals of mental illness in daytime television serials that found 11.4 percent of time in serials devoted to discussion of portrayals of mental illness; another study of restaurant critics on daily newspapers and city magazines that found such reviewers too positive in their evaluations; a study that found pre-season sports polls in football and basketball seldom correlating with end-of-season polls; and a study of movies, books, music, and adult fantasy life that found that fantasy styles showed continuity with preferred media content rather than association with a particular medium. One is moved to ask: "So what?" upon seeing such research published in the major journals of the field and to wonder about the purpose of such studies.

In fairness it should be noted that academic researchers are not the only ones producing trivial research. An Iowa Poll found two in three Iowans choosing to be reborn as themselves if reincarnation were possible and 20 percent believing in reincarnation. And an Associated Press–Media General Poll found almost half of Americans believing that intelligent life existed on other planets and half favoring the search for alien life using radio telescopes. A *Washing-*

ton Post–ABC poll reported that 54 percent of Americans didn't expect President Ronald Reagan's cancer to recur before he left office. Do such findings make a difference in what we know? Will policy makers use them in decision-making? One hopes not.

A related criticism to that of trivial research is that much mass communication research has little relationship to broad, general theories of society and social trends and to important social values. As one author put it, much American research is: "ad hoc, piecemeal and ineffective . . . totally lacking [in] any theoretical framework about the media and [their] relations to the wider society or about society itself. . . . [It tends] to analyze only one sort of effect, that on the individual, while other foci, such as effects on groups and social institutions, are omitted . . . and it is heedless of their crucial interlinkage with other social institutions."[6]

A lack of programs of research where studies build upon each other. Often, the studies published in scholarly journals of mass communication seem to have no relationship to each other and very limited links with previous studies. Replication of earlier studies is not in fashion. The Summer 1985 *Journalism Quarterly* illustrated the diversity (and lack of connection) of many studies being done in journalism and mass communication. The lead article concerned the role of religion in the John Peter Zenger case; the second looked at Senator Estes Kefauver's use of television in his crime investigation; the third dealt with a Japanese-American newspaper published in a relocation center in Arkansas in the early 1940s; the fourth reported on a nationwide telephone survey of public confidence in the news media; the fifth on source bias in Canadian TV news; the sixth on news coverage of the 1980 presidential candidates; the next on the reporting of public opinion polls from 1968 to 1984, and so on.

As one British scholar observed nearly a decade ago after looking through a number of then-recent issues of *Journalism Quarterly*, "much American material seems virtually unclassifiable . . . its social commitments and anchorages were not clearly manifest . . . the image formed in my mind of a huge, in many respects impressive, but nevertheless rather rambling, exposed and vulnerable giant."[7] This researcher did identify two strands of work where studies seemed to be related to each other—one dealing with equality of opportunity in communication (knowledge gaps, portrayal of women and minorities, etc.) and one concerned with journalistic performance (election coverage, reporter ethics, the community press, journalistic roles, etc.)—but much research seemed to be without any clear purpose.

Such diversity attests to the laissez-faire nature of academic work and to a high level of academic freedom, but it also borders on the chaotic. How can these studies add up to knowledge about journalism and mass communication if their authors are not reasonably sure of their purposes and possible contributions?

An unwillingness among many researchers to speculate upon the implications of their work for mass communication policy or practice. Aside from a few researchers who have testified before Congressional hearings on public opinion polls,[8] violence and the media,[9] or the effects of television,[10] and aside from a few who have been concerned with the application of research models and findings to news reporting,[11] it is fair to say that the majority of mass communication researchers have been too content to carry out their research, present the results at various meetings attended mostly by other researchers, and publish these results in journals and books read mostly by other researchers and students. Many scholars in political science, sociology and psychology seem to act in a similar fashion.

This apparent lack of concern on the part of many researchers for whether their studies matter to communication practitioners and policy makers was underscored by my experiences in England in 1981. There I observed various communication scholars actively involved in research concerning such issues as the sound broadcasting of the British Parliament, the purchase of *The Times* by Rupert Murdoch, and the development of the Prestel videotex system by the British Post Office. Not only were these scholars doing mass communication research that had rather clear policy implications, but they were also thrusting themselves into policy debates without waiting to be asked for their findings and opinions. It is quite common in England to see long letters to the editor in the London *Times* or the Manchester *Guardian* by researchers drawing on their studies to support positions on major issues.

This concern over the implications of research findings is related to the charge from some in the mass communication industries that much academic research is not practical. As one southern newspaper editor put it, he had never read an article in *Journalism Quarterly* that would help him put out a better newspaper.[12] This may be because he hadn't read many articles in *Journalism Quarterly* (our Gannett Foundation national survey of 1,001 American journalists indicated only 6 percent of them regularly read *JQ*),[13] but I suspect it is also because relatively few researchers take the extra time and effort to spell out the implications of their research for those working in the media and to publish these studies in places where they might be seen by practitioners and policy makers.

A confusion of statistical significance with practical significance. Too many researchers tend to equate statistically significant findings with journalistically significant ones. This is particularly common in experimental studies that analyze the differences in average scores between groups of respondents. In one research paper dealing with the social responsibility of public relations practitioners and students, a 40-point scale was used to measure degree of social responsibility, with a score of "1" indicating almost no social responsibility and a score of "40" indicating a great deal of it. The women in this study had an average score of 35.2 and the men 34.1. This difference of 1.1 points on a 40-point scale turns out to be highly significant statistically, meaning that the difference is almost sure to exist in the population from which the sample is drawn. But from such a small absolute difference, the authors conclude that women endorse more strongly than men a number of social responsibility values and that this makes sense given the traditional male upbringing in America.

My interpretation of such a slight difference, whether statistically significant or not, is that it is too small to conclude anything except that men and women public relations practitioners are very similar in social responsibility attitudes, at least as measured by this scale. There is certainly no evidence here to suggest any meaningful differences between men and women on this measure, nor is there any meaningful difference between students (34.6) and professionals (35.3), although the authors conclude that educators must develop a greater sense of social responsibility among students.

This confusion of statistical significance with practical significance can be found in numerous mass communication studies, especially those employing experimental designs.

A lack of a forum for researchers, mass communicators, and policy makers to reach and influence each other. Our 1983 national survey of 1,001 U.S. journalists from the various print and broadcast media showed that only 6 percent of them regularly read *Journalism Quarterly,* 1.5 percent regularly saw the *Newspaper Research Journal,* 5.6 percent read *Journal of Broadcasting,* 1.7 percent read *Journal of Communication,* and 3.2 percent regularly read the American Newspaper Publishers Association (ANPA) *News Research Reports.*[14] It is true that these figures increased when those who read "sometimes" were included, but the point is that very few editors, reporters, and news directors are exposed to the major sources of research on journalism and mass communication on any regular basis.

Unless the findings of the studies reported in these journals are included in *Columbia Journalism Review* (which 20 percent of U.S. journalists regularly read), *Editor & Publisher* (regularly read by 29 percent), or *The Quill* (regularly read by 18 percent), chances are that most journalists won't know about them unless they are presented at various professional meetings. Communication policy makers may be more likely to pay attention to the scholarly journals of the field, but it is clear from our national survey that most journalists do not.

Obviously, these are not the only problems with mass communication research in the United States today, but they are the ones that seem to be among the most common and serious. As with other generalizations, there are exceptions to these broad-based criticisms. There are some signs that the directions of research are changing in positive ways. In other words, there are promises as well as problems.

Promises

More and better research on journalists and media organizations. The last decade has seen an impressive increase in the number and quality of studies concentrating on the sources of media messages and the organizations producing these messages. These studies include the in-depth look at 489 newspaper journalists in eight daily newspapers by Judee K. and Michael Burgoon and Charles K. Atkin sponsored by the Newspaper Readership Project in 1981–82;[15] Stephen Hess' comprehensive study of Washington reporters for the Brookings Institution;[16] Herbert Gans' research on two network news operations (CBS and NBC) and two news magazines (*Newsweek* and *Time*);[17] the 1971 John W. C. Johnstone study of more than 1,300 U.S. journalists working for print and broadcast news media;[18] our own national study of 1,001 U.S. journalists working for print and broadcast media throughout the country; the *Los Angeles Times* study of 3,000 reporters and editors;[19] and the Associated Press Managing Editors Association survey of 1,333 daily newspaper journalists.[20]

These studies provide important insights into the backgrounds, education and training, values, attitudes, politics, ethics, professionalism, behavior, and organizational constraints of America's journalists. Some of them also begin to link the characteristics of journalists with the kinds of reports they produce, and some build upon previous studies to begin to trace trends over time (*e.g.*, Hess' study is a partial replication of Leo Rosten's well-known 1930s study of Washington correspondents,[21] and our Gannett Foundation study is a substantial replication of the Johnstone study).

Studies such as these should help journalism educators better understand the working environments of many of their former students and should help to bridge the gap between academics and professionals. While many journalists have little interest in studies of audiences, most have considerable interest in studies of themselves and their colleagues. Sometimes such studies can be critical of the way journalists do their work or the way their organizations operate, but at least these studies provide an opportunity for those in academia and the industry to exert some influence on each other.

More concern with the implications of research for communications policy and practice. Even though many researchers still care little about the implications of their research, there seem to be a growing number who do. For instance, in her research on science writers and their work, Sharon Dunwoody studied the effects of news room production pressures and the degree of interaction with other journalists on the news selection patterns of this special group of journalists.[22] She found that reporters operating under more newsroom and equipment constraints were more dependent upon others for their definitions of news. She also found that increased peer interaction generally increased the accuracy and quality of news stories. She didn't stop with these findings, however. She went on to make four specific recommendations for improving the quality of science reporting: (1) editors should not expect a story or two a day from their reporters; (2) editors should not judge their reporters' stories just in terms of what other reporters write; (3) editors should encourage specialization in a content area such as science; and (4) editors should not overemphasize competition among reporters. Whether you agree with these recommendations or not, this researcher was willing to spell out the implications of her research findings for journalistic policy and practice.

In our own studies of news coverage of the U.S. Senate, Cleve Wilhoit and I have been interested in whether the structure of the Senate is systematically linked to the frequency of news coverage of various senators, or whether the behavior of individuals is more important than organizational position in gaining news coverage.[23] We found that the activity of individual senators and their staffs was a better predictor of news coverage than was a senator's seniority or committee assignment. On the basis of this research, we recommended to The Commission on the Operation of the Senate that it not put too much stress on the development of a central staff devoted to press relations because of the tendency for reporters to seek out individual senators on the basis of their involvement in specific events and issues.

Other mass communication studies that have implications for policy are those by Guido Stempel, Peter Clarke and Eric Fredin, and Steve Chaffee and Donna Wilson on the effects of competing media voices on diversity of ideas and views in a community.[24] These studies generally find support for the proposition that competing voices in the media marketplace can increase the knowledge and variety of opinions in a community. This finding has great significance for libertarian theory, but it also relates to such communication policies as the Newspaper Preservation Act and regulations aimed at preserving competing media voices.

Still another example of research concerned with communication practice includes the Burgoon study of newspaper journalists.[25] After this research was completed, a meeting was organized by Leo Bogart of the Newspaper Advertising Bureau to discuss the implications. From that meeting came a list of possible actions that editors could take, including more opportunities for mid-career training programs for journalists, more efforts to combat isolation from the surrounding community, more written guidelines governing participation by reporters in community groups, wider reading of material produced by other kinds of writers besides journalists, more communication of readership research results to editorial staffs, and more training of journalists in the rudiments of survey research and polling.

These are not the only examples of concern with policy and practice in recent mass communication research. Recent studies include the effects of television and other media on children by Ellen Wartella and others;[26] television's coverage of elections by Jay Blumler and Michael Gurevitch;[27] and newspaper content and use by Bogart.[28]

More programs of research where studies build upon each other over time. There are signs of increasing numbers of studies that replicate earlier ones and add to our understanding of the processes and effects of mass communication. Such studies, however, still are in the minority.

The accumulation of related studies in mass communication research, as in any other field, is vital to building sound generalizations and theories and to translating research into policy and practice. One study, no matter how well done, does not carry the weight of one hundred studies carried out at different times and places and using somewhat different approaches and methods. But if these one hundred studies have almost nothing in common in the way of approaches, questions, hypotheses, concepts, and measures, they will not build upon each other in any systematic manner. In other words, it will not be possible to synthesize the results of these studies to arrive at general conclusions about the performance and effects of mass communication in our society.

Fortunately, there have been several strains of related studies emerging in mass communication research during the past decade. One of the most prolific programs of research includes the dozens of studies on the agenda-setting function of the press to which I and researchers such as Maxwell McCombs, Donald Shaw, and Doris Graber have contributed.[29] Even though many of these studies use somewhat different designs, measures, and analytic methods, most of them are similar enough that they can be roughly compared with each other and thus can yield some general conclusions about media effects. In a recent review of many of these studies, I was able to conclude that media emphasis on an issue was likely to result in increased concern over that issue by citizens, but the precise ranking of a set of issues by the media was not likely to be reflected in the rankings of these issues by individuals although the media ranking was often reflected in group rankings.[30]

Such a conclusion may seem trivial to someone not informed about mass communication research, but it is supported by more than a dozen key studies during the past decade. And it has implications for the role of mass communication in the formation of public opinion in this and other industrialized democracies. In fact, several leading forecasting firms are using agenda-setting research as a basis for predicting from media coverage which issues will be of most public concern in the weeks and months to come.

Another program of research that has resulted in a number of interrelated studies is known as cultivation theory. These studies, initiated by Dean George Gerbner of the University of Pennsylvania and his colleagues, have focused on the broad cultural effects of television in our society and have tested the notion that heavy exposure to television distorts our perceptions of the real world by causing us to overestimate and underestimate the frequency of occurrence of various events, especially acts of crime and violence.[31]

Although the results of many of these studies have been seriously questioned and hotly debated, such research does provide a series of standard measures of television content during the past two decades that is extremely valuable for detecting patterns and trends and for reaching sounder general conclusions about the amount and kind of violence presented on television.

Another area of mass communication research that has resulted in scores of related studies is the study of the effects of televised violence on aggressive behavior. Much of this research has been encouraged, if not stimulated, by funding from such government agencies as the Surgeon General's Scientific Advisory Committee on Television and Social Behavior, the National Commission on the Causes and Prevention of Violence, the National Advisory Commission on Civil Disorders, the National Science Foundation, and the National Institute of Mental Health.[32]

By systematically analyzing the results of sixty-seven important studies from 1956 to 1976, F. Scott Andison was able to conclude that there was at least a weak correlation between watching violence on television and subsequent aggression by viewers of that violence, and that television probably did stimulate a higher amount of aggression in society.[33] The 1982 National Institute of Mental Health report on television and behavior concluded that after ten more years of research (since the 1972 U.S. Surgeon General's report on the impact of televised violence) the consensus among most of the research community was that violence on television did lead to aggressive behavior by children and teenagers who watched the programs.[34] Such a conclusion would not have been possible from only a few studies but can be more confidently stated on the basis of several thousand related studies done in different times and places with different designs and methods.

Still another program of research on mass communication that has produced dozens of related—and somewhat cumulative—studies is the analysis of international news coverage. At the 1985 meeting of the Association for Education in Journalism and Mass Communication (AEJMC), a doctoral candidate from the University of Texas presented a systematic assessment of international news research for the past thirty years in which four different approaches to research were identified and critiqued. This analysis of the results of more than 150 studies identified a number of problems with past studies as well as current trends in the research, including an almost exclusive reliance on content analysis and very little study of the public's use and perceptions of foreign news.[35]

Cleve Wilhoit and I have conducted two studies of foreign news coverage in regional wire services and daily newspapers—one in 1979 and one in 1981—and I was involved in a third in 1983.[36] All of these studies used the same content categories and similar samples because we wanted to be able to track changes over time and to be able to compare our findings with those of a much larger study of foreign news coverage in twenty-nine countries sponsored by the International Association for Mass Communication Research (IAMCR) in 1978.[37]

We found that the volume of news coverage about less-developed countries was nearly equal to that about more-developed countries, but the news about Third World countries tended to focus more on conflicts and crises than did the news about more-developed countries. We also found that as one moved from the national trunk wire to the regional wire services and then to the foreign news actually used by smaller newspapers, there was a progression from a relatively rich mixture of news to a sparse, violent, conflict-laden portrait of the world in smaller newspapers—especially for Third World countries. Our 1983 study found less news dealing with conflict or crisis, especially from the Third World, and more about social problems, culture, and the arts.[38]

There are other programs of mass communication research that can be mentioned—studies of newspaper readership and circulation sponsored by the American Newspaper Publishers Association,[39] studies of the effects of advertising and pornography,[40] uses and gratifications research[41]—but the examples cited serve to illustrate both the growth and benefits of coordinated research.

More studies employing multiple methods and covering longer periods of time. The past decade has also witnessed a realization among many mass communication researchers that reliance on a single method such as the survey or the experiment often produces findings that are only part of the whole picture. As a result there is now more acceptance of a variety of methods—qualitative as well as quantitative—by many scholars than there was a decade ago. It is more common today to find research methods classes including historical, legal, and observational methods as well as the more traditional experimental, survey, and content analysis techniques. One mass communication research methods textbook recently edited by Guido Stempel and Bruce Westley includes five chapters on historical, legal, and qualitative methods.[42]

In my 1981 study of the impact of teletext and videotex technologies on the work of journalists and the flow of news in England and the Netherlands, I employed in-depth interviews, survey questionnaires, content analysis of teletext news, observation of journalists at work, and survey data from videotex users to answer my questions about the effects of this new technology.[43] Reliance on a single measure would have produced incomplete and less accurate findings.

Peter Clarke and Susan Evans used interviews with journalists, content analyses of these journalists' newspapers, and interviews with a random sample of the public to gain a more complete understanding of the nature and effects of the coverage of the 1978 congressional campaigns throughout the country.[44]

Michael MacKuen used content analysis and survey research to study the relationship between media agendas and public agendas over a seventeen-year period, as well as various "real-world" measures of unemployment, inflation, crime rates, heating fuel prices, and troop levels in Vietnam.[45]

Gladys and Kurt Lang used data from various studies, including Gallup surveys, the Opinion Research Center, Harris surveys, and the Michigan 1972 national election study to look at how Watergate became a highly salient issue to most members of the public. They concluded from a variety of evidence that heavy media coverage alone did not put Watergate at the top of the public agenda—it took the participation of other institutions, such as the courts and Congress, and the involvement of other political elites to make the issue of high concern to the public.[46]

In our year-long study of the role of newspapers and television as political agenda-setters in the 1976 presidential campaign, Maxwell McCombs, Doris Graber, and I used in-depth interviews, content analysis, and nine waves of survey interviews with the same voters to assess the effects of newspaper and television coverage on issues, images, and interest in the campaign from before the New Hampshire primary until after election day in November.[47]

And in a study of predictors of government control on the press in 134 countries from 1950 to 1979, Judith Buddenbaum, Jo Ellen Fair, and I relied on a variety of sources of information, including Arthur S. Banks' cross-polity time series data, Raymond D. Gastil's measures of civil liberties, the ITU (International Telecommunications Union) telecommunication statistics, Charles L. Taylor and Michael C. Hudson's political and social indicators, United Nations and World Bank data, as well as data analysis methods that permitted us to study relationships over this thirty-year period.[48]

Studies such as these that use multiple methods and/or longer time periods are still in the minority in mass communication research (Wilhoit found only about 5 percent using multiple methods from 1978–1980),[49] but there are signs that diversity of methods in communication studies is increasing, as Ellen Wartella and Charles Whitney have pointed out.[50] Whether diversity in methods will lead to a better understanding of mass communication is still an open question, but there is little doubt that this diversity in methods has been accompanied by a diversity in theory as well.

More debate over approaches and methods. In 1977, Jay Blumler argued in his address to the Wisconsin convention of the Association for Education in Journalism that "the spirit of scholarly debate, especially between rival traditions (of U.S. mass communication research), seems curiously muted."[51] Blumler also remarked on what he perceived as a "stultifying spirit of live and let live" among American scholars. In the eight years since Blumler's address, however, much has happened to stimulate debate over questions, approaches, and methods in mass communication research.

The publication of the Sage annual Mass Communication Review Yearbooks, beginning in 1980, has thrust European and other perspectives on communication research onto the American scene.[52] Debates over critical versus administrative research, policy versus policy-oriented studies, structuralist versus positivist approaches, and communication theory versus social theory now are much more familiar to U.S. researchers than they were a decade ago.

Another major contribution to debate over approaches and methods in mass communication research is the special Summer 1983 issue of the *Journal of Communication*, entitled "Ferment in the Field," which includes thirty-five essays by leading scholars from ten countries. This edition deals with such issues as whether communication is an academic discipline, the tension between the humanities and the social sciences in the study of communication, the debate over critical versus administrative research, and qualitative versus quantitative approaches to the study of communication.

Other developments that have increased debate and discussion about what communication research should be about include the rapid development of new communication technologies, the increasingly international membership of the International Communication Association, the rapid growth of the International Association for Mass Communication Research, and the emergence of a number of new journals outside the United States, including *Media, Culture and Society*; the *European Journal of Communication Research*; the *Canadian Journal of Communications*; and the *Keio Communication Review*.

Conclusions

The goal of this selective review has been to identify some of the major problems and promises in U.S. mass communication research and to present specific examples of both. Although many will surely disagree with my selection of problems, promises, and examples, I hope there will be some agreement among academic researchers and the professional communication community over the need to study communicators as well as messages and audiences over time to better understand the entire process of public communication. I also hope there will be some agreement that the debates over theoretical versus applied research and quantitative versus qualitative methods have served their purposes. Now we need to talk more about what kinds of *questions* should be asked than about chi-squares and green eyeshades.

Likewise, I hope that those who practice public communication will realize that those who teach and do research should be interested in developing programs of studies that lead to more general knowledge. At the same time, I hope many academic researchers will take a greater interest in the implications of their studies for communication policy and practice without becoming overly partisan or politicized and will not rely so much on measures of statistical significance as substitutes for informed judgments about practical significance. I also hope there will be more opportunities for researchers, communicators, and policy makers to communicate with each other so that the debate over approaches and methods in communication research can become more informed and useful to us all.

And I hope many communication scholars will avoid what my colleague David Nord refers to as "the two great errors of communication research"— defining communication so broadly that it loses any special meaning and trivializing communication so that an obsession with measurement and the precise specification of contingent conditions leads to "evermore narrow studies that proclaim more and more about less and less."[53] Surely, if we keep trying to ask questions whose answers make a difference, we can strike a middle ground between these two extremes that will benefit both the theory and practice of mass communication in our society.

But the burden should not be placed only on academic communication researchers. Those who control and practice mass communication must show an interest in and a willingness to support important academic research, just as those who practice in other fields do if they are to be well-informed and farsighted. There are some encouraging signs—the establishment of the Gannett Center for Media Studies to bring together academics and industry leaders, the sponsorship of important research on media credibility by the American Society of Newspaper Editors,[54] the funding of our national survey of American journalists by the Gannett Foundation, the inclusion of the news research column by Guido Stempel in the ANPA's *presstime* magazine, and the very recent survey of American daily newspaper journalists by the *Los Angeles Times*—but there is still a distance to go in establishing *programs* of worthwhile research that will lead to more informed and farsighted leadership and practice in journalism and mass communication in this country.

Such programs can provide a historical context so that the findings of each new study are not interpreted in a vacuum but rather in relation to past research on the topic. The academics can be very useful in providing such a context if the industry will support and pay attention to the research over longer periods of time than a few weeks or months. Perhaps then the promises will outweigh the problems in mass communication research.

Notes

1. For a brief review of this history, see David H. Weaver and Richard G. Gray, "Journalism and Mass Communication Research in the United States: Past, Present and Future," in G. Cleveland Wilhoit and Harold de Bock, eds., *Mass Communication Review Yearbook* 1 (Beverly Hills, Calif.: Sage Publications, 1980), 124–51.

2. Peter Golding and Graham Murdock, "Theories of Communication and Theories of Society," *Communication Research* 5 (July 1978): 339–56. Also reprinted in Wilhoit and de Bock, *Mass Communication Review Yearbook*, Volume 1, 59–76. See also Shearon Lowery and Melvin De Fleur, *Milestones in Mass Communication Research* (New York: Longman, 1983); and Ellen Wartella and Byron Reeves, "Historical Trends in Research on Children and the Media: 1900–1960," *Journal of Communication* 35 (Spring 1985): 118–33.

3. Weaver and Gray, "Journalism and Mass Communication Research," 142.

4. John C. Schweitzer, "Practical research can bring respect to J-schools," *Journalism Educator* 40 (Summer 1985): 38–41.

5. Peter Clarke, "How Much of Communication Research Is Worth Knowing About?" *T&M Newsletter* of the Association for Education in Journalism and Mass Communication (December 1973): 5.

6. Annabelle Sreberny-Mohammadi, "Television and Its Effects: A Reconstruction of the Ditchley Conference," *Communications and Development* 1 (Spring 1977): 8–10, as quoted in Jay G. Blumler, "Purposes of Mass Communications Research: A Transatlantic Perspective," *Journalism Quarterly* 55 (Summer 1978): 226.

7. Blumler, "Purposes of Research," 225.

8. Committee on House Administration, *Public Opinion Polls: Hearings before the Subcommittee on Libraries and Memorials on H.R. 5003* (Washington, D.C.: U.S. Government Printing Office, 1973).

9. Robert K. Baker and Sandra J. Ball, *Violence and the Media: A Staff Report to the National*

Commission on the Causes and Prevention of Violence (Washington, D.C.: U.S. Government Printing Office, 1969).

10. U.S. Senate Subcommittee on Communications, *Surgeon General's Report by the Scientific Advisory Committee on Television and Social Behavior* (Washington, D.C.: U.S. Government Printing Office, 1972); U.S. Senate Subcommittee on Communications, *Hearings on the Surgeon General's Report by the Scientific Advisory Committee on Television and Social Behavior* (Washington, D.C.: U.S. Government Printing Office, 1972); House Committee on Interstate and Foreign Commerce, Hearings before the Subcommittee on Communications, *Broadcast Advertising and Children* (Washington, D.C.: U.S. Government Printing Office, 1976).

11. Maxwell E. McCombs, "A New Focus for Research: Applying Social Science Methodology to News Reporting," *T&M Newsletter* of the Association for Education in Journalism and Mass Communication (December 1975): 7–10; Maxwell E. McCombs and Lee B. Becker, *Using Mass Communication Theory* (Englewood Cliffs, N.J.: Prentice-Hall, 1979); and David H. Weaver and Maxwell E. McCombs, "Journalism and Social Science: A New Relationship?" *Public Opinion Quarterly* 44 (Winter 1980): 477–94.

12. Schweitzer, "Practical research," 39.

13. David H. Weaver and G. Cleveland Wilhoit, *The American Journalist: A Portrait of U.S. News People and Their Work* (Bloomington: Indiana University Press, 1986), 110–11.

14. Weaver and Wilhoit, *The American Journalist,* 110.

15. Judee K. Burgoon, Michael Burgoon, and Charles K. Atkin, *The World of the Working Journalist* (New York: Newspaper Advertising Bureau, 1982).

16. Stephen Hess, *The Washington Reporters* (Washington, D.C.: The Brookings Institution, 1982).

17. Herbert J. Gans, *Deciding What's News* (New York: Vintage, 1980).

18. John W. C. Johnstone, Edward J. Slawski, and William W. Bowman, *The News People* (Urbana: University of Illinois Press, 1976).

19. David Shaw, "Public and Press—Two Viewpoints," Los Angeles *Times,* August 11, 1985.

20. Associated Press Managing Editors, "Journalists and Readers: Bridging the Credibility Gap." This 1985 report is available from Robert Ritter, executive editor of the San Bernardino, Calif., *Sun.*

21. Leo Rosten, *The Washington Correspondents* (New York: Harcourt, Brace and Co., 1937).

22. Sharon Dunwoody, "Science Writers at Work," Center for New Communications Research Report No. 7 (Bloomington, Indiana: School of Journalism, 1978); see also Sharon Dunwoody, "Science Journalists: A Study of Factors Affecting the Selection of News at a Scientific Meeting," doctoral dissertation, Indiana University, December 1978.

23. David H. Weaver and G. Cleveland Wilhoit, "News Media Coverage of U.S. Senators in Four Congresses, 1953–1974," *Journalism Monographs* 67 (April 1980): 1–34. See also David H. Weaver, G. Cleveland Wilhoit, Sharon Dunwoody, and Paul Hagner, "Senatorial News Coverage: Agenda-Setting for Mass and Elite Media in the U.S.," *Senate Communications with the Public* (Washington, D.C.: U.S. Government Printing Office, 1977).

24. Peter Clarke and Eric Fredin, "Newspapers, Television, and Political Reasoning," *Public Opinion Quarterly* 43 (Summer 1978): 143–60; Steven H. Chaffee and Donna Wilson, "Media Rich, Media Poor: Two Studies of Diversity in Agenda-Holding," *Journalism Quarterly,* 54 (Autumn 1977): 466–76; and Guido H. Stempel III, "Effects on Performance of a Cross-Media Monopoly," *Journalism Monographs* 29 (June 1973).

25. Burgoon, Burgoon, and Atkin, "World of Journalist."

26. Wartella and Reeves, "Historical Trends in Research"; Mabel L. Rice, Aletha C. Hus-

ton, and John C. Wright, "The Forms of Television: Effects on Children's Attention, Comprehension, and Social Behavior," in National Institute of Mental Health, *Television and Behavior: Ten Years of Scientific Progress and Implications for the Eighties* 2 (Rockville, Maryland: National Institute of Mental Health, 1982), 24–38, reprinted in Ellen Wartella and D. Charles Whitney, eds., *Mass Communication Review Yearbook* 4 (Beverly Hills, Calif.: Sage Publications, 1983), 37–51.

27. Jay G. Blumler and Denis McQuail, *Television in Politics* (Chicago: University of Chicago Press, 1968); Jay G. Blumler, Michael Gurevitch, and Julian Ives, *The Challenge of Election Broadcasting* (Leeds, U.K.: Leeds University Press, 1978); and Michael Gurevitch and Jay Blumler, "The Construction of Election News: An Observation Study at the BBC," in James S. Ettema and D. Charles Whitney, eds., *Individuals in Mass Media Organizations* (Beverly Hills, Calif.: Sage Publications, 1982), 179–204.

28. Leo Bogart, *Press and Public* (Hillsdale, New Jersey: Lawrence Erlbaum, 1981); Leo Bogart, "How U.S. Newspaper Content is Changing," *Journal of Communication* 35 (Spring 1985): 82–90; and Leo Bogart, "The Public's Use and Perception of Newspapers," *Public Opinion Quarterly* 48 (Winter 1984–85), 709–19.

29. David H. Weaver, Doris A. Graber, Maxwell E. McCombs, and Chaim H. Eyal, *Media Agenda-Setting in a Presidential Election: Issues, Images and Interest* (New York: Praeger, 1981); David H. Weaver, "Media Agenda-Setting and Public Opinion: Is There a Link?" in Robert N. Bostrom, ed., *Communication Yearbook* 8 (Beverly Hills, Calif.: Sage Publications, 1984), 680–91; David H. Weaver and Swanzy Nimley Elliott, "Who Sets the Agenda for the Media? A Study of Local Agenda-Building," *Journalism Quarterly* 62 (Spring 1985): 87–94; and Maxwell E. McCombs and David H. Weaver, "Toward a Merger of Gratifications and Agenda-Setting Research," in Karl Erik Rosengren, Lawrence A. Wenner, and Philip Palmgreen, eds., *Media Gratifications Research: Current Perspectives* (Beverly Hills, Calif.: Sage Publications, 1985), 95–108.

30. Weaver, "Media Agenda-Setting and Public Opinion."

31. See Part V, "Crime and Violence in Mass Communication," in Wilhoit and de Bock, eds., *Mass Communication Review Yearbook* 1, 401–88, for a collection of articles describing and reacting to Gerbner and colleagues' research on television's depiction of violence. See also various issues of *Journal of Communication* for reports of this research.

32. For major reviews of these studies, see the National Institute of Mental Health, *Television and Behavior: Ten Years of Scientific Progress and Implications for the Eighties* 1 (Rockville, Maryland: National Institute of Mental Health, 1982); George Comstock *et al.*, *Television and Human Behavior* (New York: Columbia University Press, 1978); and F. Scott Andison, "TV Violence and Viewer Agression: A Cumulation of Study Results 1956–1976," *Public Opinion Quarterly* 41 (Fall 1977): 314–31.

33. Andison, "TV Violence."

34. National Institute of Mental Health, *Television and Behavior.*

35. Kuo-jen Tsang, "International News Communication Research: A Meta-Analytic Assessment," paper presented to the International Communication Division, Association for Education in Journalism and Mass Communication annual convention, Memphis, Tennessee, August 3–6, 1985.

36. David H. Weaver and G. Cleveland Wilhoit, "Foreign News Coverage in Two U.S. Wire Services," *Journal of Communication* 31 (Spring 1981): 55–63; G. Cleveland Wilhoit and David H. Weaver, "Foreign News Coverage in Two U.S. Wire Services: An Update," *Journal of Communication* 33 (Spring 1983): 132–48; and Mohamed Kirat and David Weaver, "Foreign News Coverage in Three Wire Services: A Study of AP, UPI, and the Nonaligned News Agencies Pool," *Gazette* 35, no. 1 (1985): 31–47.

37. Annabelle Sreberny-Mohammadi, Kaarle Nordenstreng, Robert Stevenson, and Frank Ugboajah, "Foreign News in the Media: International Reporting in 29 Countries," *UNESCO Reports and Papers on Mass Communication,* No. 93 (1985).

38. Wilhoit and Weaver, "Foreign News Coverage"; Kirat and Weaver, "Foreign News Coverage."

39. See ANPA News Research Reports, nos. 1–40, as well as *News Research for Better Newspapers* 1–7 (Washington, D.C.: American Newspaper Publishers Association, 1964–1979). Unfortunately, the American Newspaper Publishers Association has discontinued this program of research at a time when other organizations, such as the American Society of Newspaper Editors and the Associated Press Managing Editors, are sponsoring important research on journalists and their work.

40. For a readable and concise summary of many of these studies, see Everette E. Dennis, *The Media Society: Evidence About Mass Communication in America* (Dubuque, Iowa: Wm. C. Brown, 1978), 21–30. Also see Scott Ward, Daniel B. Wackman and Ellen Wartella, *Children Learning to Buy: The Development of Consumer Information Processing Skills* (Beverly Hills, Calif.: Sage Publications, 1977) and *The Report of the Commission on Obscenity and Pornography,* New York *Times* Edition (New York: Bantam Books, 1970).

41. The most recent review of these studies is Karl Erik Rosengren, Lawrence A. Wenner, and Philip Palmgreen, eds., *Media Gratifications Research: Current Perspectives* (Beverly Hills, Calif.: Sage Publications, 1985). Another important review is Jay G. Blumler and Elihu Katz, eds., *The Uses of Mass Communications: Current Perspectives on Gratifications Research* (Beverly Hills, Calif.: Sage Publications, 1974).

42. Guido H. Stempel III and Bruce H. Westley, *Research Methods in Mass Communication* (Englewood, Cliffs, N.J.: Prentice-Hall, 1981).

43. David H. Weaver, *Videotex Journalism: Teletext, Viewdata, and the News* (Hillsdale, N.J.: Lawrence Erlbaum, 1983).

44. Peter Clarke and Susan H. Evans, *Covering Campaigns: Journalism in Congressional Elections* (Stanford, California: Stanford University Press, 1983).

45. Michael B. MacKuen and Steven L. Coombs, *More Than News: Media Power in Public Affairs* (Beverly Hills, Calif.: Sage Publications, 1981).

46. Gladys Engle Lang and Kurt Lang, "Watergate: An Exploration of the Agenda-Building Process," in Wilhoit and de Bock, *Mass Communication Review Yearbook,* vol. 1.

47. Weaver, Graber, McCombs, and Eyal, *Media Agenda-Setting in a Presidential Election.*

48. David H. Weaver, Judith M. Buddenbaum, and Jo Ellen Fair, "Press Freedom, Media, and Development, 1950–1979: A Study of 134 Nations," *Journal of Communication* 35 (Spring 1985): 104–17.

49. Wilhoit and de Bock, *Mass Communication Review Yearbook* 2 (Beverly Hills, Calif.: Sage Publications, 1980), 14.

50. D. Charles Whitney and Ellen Wartella, eds., *Mass Communication Review Yearbook* 3 (Beverly Hills, Calif.: Sage Publications, 1982), 15–16.

51. Jay G. Blumler, "Purposes of Mass Communications Research: A Transatlantic Perspective," *Journalism Quarterly* 55 (Summer 1978): 226, reprinted in Wilhoit and de Bock, *Mass Communication Review Yearbook* 1.

52. Wilhoit and de Bock, eds., *Mass Communication Review Yearbook,* vols. 1 and 2; Whitney and Wartella, eds., *Mass Communication Review Yearbook,* vols. 3 and 4.

53. David Paul Nord, "Career Narrative," Unpublished Memorandum, September 30, 1985, 1.

54. American Society of Newspaper Editors, *Newspaper Credibility: Building Reader Trust* (Washington, D.C.: ASNE, 1985).

Where Is Mass Communication Research Going?

Frederick T. C. Yu

Forecasting is a risky business, but it can be fun. There is a special foolhardiness in accepting an invitation to predict where mass communication research is going. But the invitation activates one's Walter Mittyism – the dream that one may even discover a brave new world of mass communication research. And so we proceed down the road from forecast to fantasy.

I approach this assignment with three assumptions:

• Mass communication research, like all fields of study, is defined by what it does; its future will be decided by what problems it will study, how it will study them, and what it will learn.

• What will happen in this field of study will depend more on what will happen in the media and related academic disciplines and on what the media and society will do to each other than on what has happened in academic communication research institutions.

• The study of mass communication presents a special problem that is in need of rethinking. We have entered an unprecedented era of explosive technological developments and continuing social changes. Accelerating advances in the field of communication and information are changing not only the mass media but also the way we communicate, work, live, and organize our society. These developments and changes raise important questions about many of the ideas, methods, and institutions that have guided the study of mass communication during the past thirty or forty years. They present exciting opportunities and pose enormous challenges for mass communication researchers.

Taking Stock

We should have a solid understanding of this field before we can speculate about where it is going or suggest where it should be going. This is easy to say but difficult to do. Mass communication research has grown so fast and expanded into so many specialties in so many directions that it is difficult to get a clear and complete picture of the entire field. Even researchers have trouble keeping track of developments within their own specialties. Just how many specialties and sub-specialties are there in this field? How many and what kinds of researchers are doing how much and what kinds of research about what kinds of problems in what kinds of institutions? We don't really know.

Some of these specialties, such as consumer and opinion research, have acquired identities of their own. Some, such as advertising research, started long before mass communication became a subject of study. Some emerging specialties, such as communication policy research, are barely recognizable. Of course, not all specialties are equally productive. Those with larger memberships do not necessarily produce more research than those with fewer practitioners.

Take the vast proliferated area of international communication research. Ithiel de Sola Pool observed:

> There is, in fact, remarkably little research of any kind of international communication. There is a great deal of essay writing about it. But by research I mean studies in which data is collected to establish or refute some general proposition. . . .
>
> The two topics regarding international communication that have been most extensively studied, and very badly, I must say, are the balance in the flow of communication among countries, and the cultural biases in what flows. Those are topics on which there have been a few empirical studies, though by far the great bulk of that literature consists of polemical essays unenlightened by facts.[1]

Pool illustrated this point with the book, *National Sovereignty and International Communications*, edited by Kaarle Nordenstreng and Herbert Schiller. He went on:

> [N]ot one of the papers was a research study of the kind that social scientists normally do. A couple of the papers reviewed some social science literature and cited empirical examples, but use of social science or quoting of empirical data is not the same thing as *doing* research. I say this not to claim that

every book is obligated to be a social science research study; there are other legitimate activities in the world too. But I cite this book since most of us authors are social scientists, and it is, I fear, typical rather than exceptional in the literature about international communication.[2]

There are good reasons for us to focus our attention on what prominent researchers such as Pool have considered to be serious and solid international communication research by social scientists—that is, carefully designed research projects on well defined international communication problems, carefully stated concepts and theories, and carefully tested propositions and findings about such problems, and not simply opinions, insights, and advice of social scientists. There are equally good reasons to believe that Pool's definition covers only one type of research and that international communication research—or mass communication research for that matter—is by no means limited to social science research.

Much of the talk about mass communication research dwells on the work of a special group of academic communication scholars. Most of them teach in communication departments or journalism schools, direct graduate communication programs, supervise doctoral dissertations in communication, and publish in communication journals. This is a fast-growing community. In the days of what Wilbur Schramm has called the "Founding Fathers" of mass communication research, only a handful of communication doctorates were awarded in any year. In 1984, according to the Spring 1985 issue of *Journalism Educator*, 540 doctoral students were enrolled in departments and schools of communication and journalism in the United States. Minnesota headed the list with fifty students in its doctoral program, but Iowa and Southern Illinois awarded the most doctorates, each reporting eight in 1984. In the 1940s and 1950s only a handful of communication journals existed. Schramm counted about fifty in 1983. In the 1940s the annual publication of journal articles and books was a little more than a hundred. In 1982, according to Schramm, "a thousand articles and book chapters were summarized at length in a single quarterly publication called *Communication Abstracts*, and these were chosen selectively rather than inclusively."[3]

It is hard to characterize these academic mass communication researchers and still harder to determine their role. They are growing perhaps faster in number than in status. They are distinguished perhaps more by what they are than what they do. Because of their positions, they probably play a more important role in journalism education than mass communication research. Most of them are products of graduate programs in communication and journalism although a significantly large number of them are trained in the social sciences and related disciplines.

They seem to operate in a world of their own. They establish their own journals, organize their own associations, and publish in their own journals and yearbooks. They have become increasingly more independent of various academic disciplines and related professions and, at the same time, more isolated.

Schramm, who knows the work of this group of researchers better than most students of mass communication research, observed recently that the fast growth rate of this group "is at once reassuring and worrisome" because "it is inevitable in a field developing as fast as this one that a great deal of trivia and a relatively small proportion of truly insightful research will be published."[4]

Jeremy Tunstall, a noted British media sociologist, has a more critical view of U.S. mass communication research. He probably had these academic communication researchers in mind when he wrote that "something is badly wrong with U.S. communication research" and that "the symptoms include too much low-quality work and very little, if any, work of really high quality." The "central disease," to him, is fragmentation. He went on:

> The fragmentation that is U.S. communication studies takes many forms. I believe the central mistake was to have a discipline on a combination of practical journalism and social psychology. The fact that a single individual can teach courses in, say, magazine editing and research techniques in social psychology is a tribute to human adaptability, not a well-conceived academic discipline.
>
> Once a field becomes fragmented and acquires a reputation for low-quality research, it becomes hard to attract or retain people of the highest quality. The old pattern of the researchers passing by, but not staying, will continue. In such a fragmented field, reputation is also fragmented – in other words, even if you do superior work, the quality may not be recognized.[5]

This is not a new criticism of mass communication research. The field has received even harsher criticism not only from social scientists but also from scholars in other disciplines, professionals in the media, and journalism educators. Among the familiar criticisms: much communication research lacks direction, much of it is neither intellectually exciting nor socially useful, and little either commands very high respect in academia or enjoys wide support from the profession of journalism.

But to be fair to academic communication researchers we should set the record straight and make two important points: (1) their work constitutes only one part of this vast and still largely uncharted field of mass communication research; and (2) their research environment is quite different from what it was thirty or forty years ago.

Many scholars (not just social scientists) and writers who work on mass communication problems are not associated with communication departments or journalism schools. Some work in other academic departments or schools in universities. Others are employed by the news media, advertising agencies, consumer research companies, opinion research and survey centers, consulting firms, government offices, and world organizations. Some publish in journals of their academic disciplines and some in trade organs. Some do research for their clients. Many are in mass communication research as a business.

The emerging communication policy research, for instance, is a fragmented preserve of disparate experts. Researchers in this new specialty carry very different tool bags that are arbitrarily filled with instruments and instructions from law, economics, engineering, political science, sociology, and business. Not many are conventional mass communication researchers. A leading scholar in this area was Pool. But he was no conventional communication researcher. Another important figure in the field is Edwin Parker, formerly of the Institute of Communication Research at Stanford. He has left academia.

When Paul Lazarsfeld entered mass communication research, he introduced survey research to the field. He founded the Bureau of Applied Social Research at Columbia University. Then came the Survey Research Center at Michigan and the Social Science Research Center at Chicago. During those early days survey research had a special place of importance in graduate communication programs, and it attracted media attention and support. Much of Lazarsfeld's research at Columbia, for instance, was supported by CBS. Some of the early public opinion polls were conducted by university researchers. Today, a great deal of survey research is done by media organizations themselves and some can be bought from commercial research firms. The polls of CBS and the *New York Times* have become regular operations. More than one hundred survey centers are based in universities and, according to Eleanor Singer, editor of *Public Opinion Quarterly*, at least one hundred media organizations have their own research units.

In 1959, when mass communication research was still a relatively new field of study, Bernard Berelson wrote that "the state is withering away."[6] In 1972 Herbert H. Gans wrote about "the famine in mass communication research"[7] although eleven years later he talked about "the study of news and the news media" as "one of the liveliest fields within communication research."[8] Schramm described the state of affairs in the early days with that much-quoted statement that communication research was "an academic crossroad where many have passed but few have tarried."[9] Schramm now sees things a little differently, speaking of communication research as "a new academic oasis" where a new type of research scholar has moved in and settled down. But Schramm wonders whether the new settlers can really build something stable except upon the foundation of an old and honored discipline.[10]

Perhaps the metaphors of "an academic crossroad" and "a new academic oasis" are not quite appropriate. Both suggest a place, something spatial and stationary. A map of mass communication research does not yet exist; but, if one were to draw such a map, this "crossroad" or "oasis" would be just a spot or region on it. Furthermore, it is hard to picture communication research as an "oasis," which is defined in dictionaries as a fertile or green area in an arid region or something providing relief from boring or dreary routine. To be sure, many settlers—those new Ph.D.s in communications—have moved in to settle down, but some settlers do move on to other regions that are even greener and more fertile.

Perhaps we should look at mass communication research simply as a field of study, something like international relations or area studies. It can be compared with the study of engineering, medicine, law, business, technology, or environment. It requires the work of scholars of many skills from many disciplines.

It is perhaps fitting to think of mass communication research as a caravan on an intellectual expedition. This caravan has traveled some distance and traversed many crossroads. It is now at another crossroad. It has to know where it *is* going and where it *should be* going.

Future Directions

We can answer the two questions by raising two other questions: "What problems are likely to be studied?" "What problems should be studied?"

We know some answers to the first question. We can expect more research on most of the problems in the field. Every specialty in mass communication research has its research agenda. Certain problems are the main concerns of certain specialties, and some specialties are more concerned with methodological than substantive problems.

There was a time when advertising and commercial research was confined to newspapers, magazines, and radio, and much of the research had to do with the learning and forgetting of advertising messages. Then television developed and introduced changes in research. And new advertising media created still more changes. But the measurement of advertising effects is still the main concern of this specialized area of research. "The agenda of unanswered questions in advertising and commercial research," Leo Bogart noted in 1973, "continues to remain almost identical with those that face the academic student of communication and persuasion."[11]

Opinion research, which deals with all kinds of opinions that can be measured, is always concerned with measurement techniques and methodological problems. It seeks constantly to develop new and better methods of opinion and survey research. For instance, when AAPOR (American Association of Public Opinion Research) and WAPOR (World Association of Public Opinion Research) planned a joint convention in 1986, high on their agenda was, as always, the problem of methodological development. They called for papers dealing with validation studies (comparison of surveys and other measurement techniques for determining TV ratings, readership, trends in the economy, etc.); indirect survey estimation techniques (randomized responses, normative techniques, shadow weights); experimental design (studies of response rate and question wording); telephone interviews (how to get more out of the technique, compromises versus innovations in telephone survey design); developments in the design and use of mail surveys; qualitative research techniques; finding and questioning rare and hard-to-reach populations (the homeless, millionaires, low incident product users); mathematical models of public opinion dynamics; new developments and applications of choice models (treatment of uncertainty, variety-seeking, etc.); physiological measurement techniques; and popular culture as an indicator of public opinion. Also scheduled were papers on professional developments and concerns of public opinion researchers, including the problems of research and the law (researchers as expert witnesses, conflicts faced when research findings are used for advocacy); research entrepreneurs (the academic as research entrepreneur and research as a business); pending legislation that would affect survey research; and critical decisions based on survey research (case histories in marketing, elections, public policy).

Instead of considering research concerns of various specialties, let us look at the entire field of mass communication research. What ideas and problems should be called onto the research stage?

Nearly fifteen years ago W. Phillips Davison and I organized a research conference to ponder this question. We produced a volume on the major issues and future directions of mass communication research with contributions by Ben H. Bagdikian, Jay Blumler, Leo Bogart, Davis B. Bobrow, Michael Gurevitch, Herbert Hyman, Elihu Katz, Daniel Lerner, and Edwin B. Parker.[12] Our guiding question was: What kinds of knowledge are necessary if societies are to make rational decisions regarding the organization and operation of the mass media? We raised several complexes of questions for research: What social and individual needs can the mass media help to satisfy? What is the preferred relationship, for each society, between mass communication and interpersonal channels? What types of media and content are best suited to what kinds of tasks? How can standards of mass media performance be defined? How can the media confer the greatest benefits at the lowest cost? These questions remain as important and almost as fresh as the day they were proposed.

A Simple Model

Davison and I found it necessary to structure the field of mass communication research in order to identify the principal areas for research and the principal tasks of researchers. We started with a simple model of communication in society, one that links individuals and collectivities in two-way communication channels (the two lines indicate two-way communication):

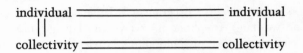

We then added the mass media, which introduced new dimensions in this model:

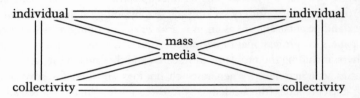

This model linking mass media with individuals and with collectivities indicates certain basic processes of communication and presents three principal areas for research: (1) relationships between the individual and the mass media, (2) relationships between social organizations and the mass media, and (3) the way these relationships interact with communication mechanisms and technologies to result in the formation of particular types of message content.

This model remains useful today as a device to indicate the types of processes or relationships in which the mass media are involved, to see how much and what mass communication research has learned about what kinds of processes or relationships, and to suggest what research is needed to improve our understanding of other processes or relationships.

U.S. Media System

Questions to be explored. What sorts of problems should be on the agenda for future research? The following are proposed as starters.

Let's start with the basic: the U.S. media system.

The problem: What kind of media system do we have in the United

States? How well is this system meeting individual and societal needs? How would it better serve these needs?

These are several sets of specific questions to be explored:

• How is this system structured now? How does it function? How has it changed?

• Who owns what in this system? What is the pattern of media ownership? How is the pattern changing? Who are the new owners? What does it take to own what in this system? How are investments in media related to other investments in the financial community? What determines how media profits are reinvested in the system or in other enterprises? What do we know about the joint ventures, mergers, takeovers, and new services?

• Who runs what in the system? And how? What new knowledge do we need about media management and media operations?

• How do the changes in the three main areas of the system—information, entertainment, and advertising—converge? What effect does this have on the system?

• Who wants, needs, gets, and uses what this system has to offer?

• What is the role of the system in the shaping of values and behavioral patterns? What do we know about the communication of values?

• What do we know and what should we know about the various types of media workers, their performance, and their problems? How is their performance evaluated? How should it be evaluated?

• What is the impact of technological changes on the system? What are the directions and dimensions of these changes?

• What is this system doing *to* and *for* our political, economic, and cultural environments? How is it shaped or reshaped by these environments?

• What is the role of this system in the world society?

• Who can do what to make this system work better and be more responsive to people's needs?

Forecasting. A critical test of how well we study and understand a system is our ability to predict or forecast its behavior. For instance, understanding the atmosphere and the solar system enables meteorologists to make weather forecasts and to predict such happenings as sunrises, eclipses, and comet movements. Similarly, understanding the political system and the voting process allows pollsters to make election forecasts. While meteorologists and pollsters are not always accurate, they have made progress in their studies, developed better tools and techniques, and improved their abilities to predict.

The system as a whole. We are still a long way from completely understanding our media system, and we don't know nearly as much as we should in order to attempt much significant forecasting. Americans know many things and have very definite ideas about different parts of this system, but not many of them understand the system as a whole. The subject has not even received much serious attention from media researchers. Conventional communication researchers still are concerned mainly with specific topics of the Lasswellian "who-says-what-in-which-channel-to-whom-with-what-effect" question. They seem to be much more interested in how people in a nation behave in a media system than in what a nation could or should do with its media system. Many parts of this system are heavily studied and widely debated. Some studies explore one medium, such as public television, while others examine one kind of content, such as TV sex or violence. Some analyze one kind of coverage, such as foreign news, and some aim at discerning one or another of the particular effects of one kind of news or advertising on one kind of consumer or one part of a community. But systematic inquiries into the entire media system are rare.

On the other hand, is it really important to study the entire media system? Is it really necessary to predict its future? Who really knows what the system will look like thirty or forty years hence? How predictable was our present media system thirty or forty years ago? Who predicted at the end of World War II an American media system that included television, 24-hour cable TV news, videodisc, video cassette recorders, teletext, videotex, subscription TV, and direct broadcast satellites? Who forecast an information environment made up of such fanciful things as microwaves, laser beams, data bits, microcomputer chips, satellites, digital wires, fiber optics, memory banks, word processors, personal computers, teleconferencing, teleshopping, telebanking, and tele-almost-anything?

An obvious answer to these questions is that forecasting is inherent in all system evaluations and public policy research. A somewhat less obvious—but equally important—answer is the premise that the media system we will have depends to a certain extent on what we desire, demand, or do. Forecasting the future of our media system is not quite the same as predicting tomorrow's weather. Meteorologists may predict the weather accurately, but they can't really do anything about it. Our forecast of the media system may be nowhere near as certain, but we can do something about it. Obviously, the system may not always go the way we want it to. But the emphasis should be on thinking ahead, on knowing the options, and on making policies and plans. This is where research is needed.

Meeting needs. To ask how the media system is meeting our individual and societal needs and how it would better serve these needs is to evaluate the performance of the system and to recommend ways for its improvement. We are in effect asking: Is the media system doing what it is supposed to do and working as well as it is supposed to work?

We do not have many evaluative standards and tools for answering this question. We do not even agree on ways to arrive at standards. Journalists receive prizes and awards for good work. They know the elements of journalistic excellence, but they cannot always explain to outsiders what these elements are. This is an area where social scientists and journalists run into some predictable troubles when they discuss communication research on journalistic performance.

Gans, for instance, talks about "an urgent 'in house' task for news policy research: the development of criteria for judging and evaluating the news," because all too often the judgements of news researchers tend to reflect "criteria and standards of one or another version of the scientific methods which cannot be the only, or even the major, standard setters for journalism." Gans thinks that news media researchers with an interest in policy must begin to propose and discuss other norms with which to evaluate the news. This is, of course, a very difficult venture. On the other hand, to quote Gans again, "only if we give serious and systematic thoughts to news norms and news media purposes do we have the right to tell journalists and others whether and how to improve the news."[13]

Information environments. It is easy to ask how well the media system is meeting the needs of our society and how it could better serve those needs. However, this question cannot be answered now because we have yet to gain a clear understanding of how these needs are perceived by those in the media and how the media system functions in the total information environment.

Most media studies offer one-dimensional views on this environment and this system. Not many studies examine the way in which people use all channels of information and entertainment available to them and how they compare, integrate, weigh, and recall information and entertainment from multiple sources. We know that information, entertainment, and advertising grow together in this system, but how the three functions interact is dimly understood and little studied. Research on news media rarely deals with entertainment. Few studies of entertainment have much to do with information. And advertising researchers concentrate on doing their own thing.

Consider, for instance, a few television programs. Such early network programs as ABC's "Good Morning America" and the "CBS Morning News" have had news and information as their basic text and format but have used many show-biz presentation techniques. On the other hand, such entertainment shows as "That's Incredible" and "Real People" can be very informative. Home video cassette recorders have changed the way many families spend their leisure time with television and other media. They have given rise to a new industry, led television networks to consider new programming services, and encouraged more making and viewing of home movies. The claims by telephone and computer companies that they are entering the "information business" and the "knowledge business" are not just cute or empty advertising slogans. But how do all these fit into the media system?

Pool looked at the challenge for research and wrote:

> If there is to be a new wave of exciting research on communication, it is likely to be on new questions made salient by drastic changes in the communication situation. While we can expect to make some marginal progress in understanding the effects of the mass media, I see no reason to anticipate a major breakthrough in this area. But new technologies raise different questions than do the mass media. For example, because mass media are one-way, controlled by a small population of producers and consumed in the same form by millions of people, we are naturally curious about the "effects" of such heavy stimuli. . . .
>
> But this is not the salient question to ask about an information retrieval system. If people have access to an enormous range of information and are able to choose what they want out of it, they may have all sorts of problems in skill and motivation in finding just what they want, but no one is telling them what ought to be heard or seen. This situation makes the user more interesting than the effects of the messages on that user. We are likely to see interesting research being done on people's motivation to seek knowledge, on their styles of search, on their gains of knowledge, and on their creativity in learning, as well as on how they interact with one another when each retrieves different information.[14]

Understanding the impact of technological changes is a much trickier research problem than we generally realize. Edwin B. Parker alerted us to one aspect of this problem during the early years of communication policy research:

> Much research needs to be done to bring to fruition the social potential of the new communication technology and to determine the possible benefits and dangers before the technology has been widely adopted. The major studies of the effects of television (Himmelweit, Oppenheim, and Vince, 1958; Schramm, Lyle, and Parker, 1961) were completed after television had been widely diffused through the society. This was some twenty years after the television became publicly available. By the time the studies were completed, it was too late to change the technology, and, at least in the United States, too late to change the economic and regulatory structure of the television industry in anything except very minor ways.[15]

Parker made this point even more sharply in another piece:

> If we structure the problem [of technology assessment] as one of assessment of the technology itself, or as one of the developing social indicators to better measure social effects after they have happened, then the battle will have been lost before we start. By the time we have definitive measures of social effects, the political, economic, and institutional structure surrounding the new technology will be well entrenched and highly resistant to change.[16]

Pool was talking about another aspect of this problem when he wrote:

> Researchers tend to look at the wave that has passed. Students of international communication are no exception. . . . This is to some extent inevitable. It was as true of classics of social science as it is of inferior works. . . . So we do not have to be ashamed of the fact that most of the current research on international communication, which authors believe deals with its structure, is in fact about the old structure that is rapidly passing. Since most researchers are not in the class of Marx, or Weber, or Keynes, more often than not they are writing about a wave that is not about to pass in a decade or two, but that is already well past. . . .[17] [T]he existing literature does not deal with the most significant and interesting developments in international communications today. It deals with the extraordinary explosion of international mass communication that occurred some two or three decades ago, most notably with the coming of the transistor radio and then television.[18]

The U.S. media system is, of course, larger and more complex than it used to be. It includes new media as well as old media doing new things. Cable has evolved from a way to improve television reception in the late 1940s to a new mass medium, now reaching almost 50 percent of U.S. households and already facing competition from many new over-the-air services. Newspapers have become electronic, and more and more of them have been absorbed into ever-growing chains and multi-interest corporations. Radio stations increasingly have become units in larger economic concentrations, and FM-radio has become a medium of narrowcasting appealing to highly specialized interests. Neither telephone nor television is new, but both are doing new things. A television set used to be just a receiver; it now has multiple functions. It even "watches" us. Computers and satellites aren't exactly new, either. What is new is the merging of telephone, television, computers, satellites, and many other communications devices into a single, yet differentiated, system that allows the transmission of information and data between persons or computers through cables, microwave relays, or satellites.

It was not very long ago that mass communication researchers could completely ignore telecommunications and leave all technical questions to engineers and regulatory problems to lawyers. The convergence of modes of communication has raised new and difficult questions for all Americans. Questions such as cable connections and backyard earth stations in a community have become concerns of common citizens. There are, of course, many more complicated communications policy questions than these. For instance, would increasing electrification of print technology lead to more government regulation of the press with attendant dangers to our civil liberties? Or would the increasingly maturing electronic communications allow for more pluralism, diversity, and absence of regulation than the traditional print media ever did?

A change in "mass-ness." We still speak of mass communication, but the "mass-ness" has changed. New information technologies have enabled newspapers and magazines to have demographic editions for different masses. Various types of viewdata systems can allow individuals to create the types of information packages that they want although the development of such systems is still limited by practical economics.

This is perhaps a good place to bring up another communication research area. It is what Herbert Menzel calls "Quasi-Mass Communication: A Neglected Area." This is that vast area setting the dichotomy of mass communication and person-to-person communication. This dichotomization, he writes, "leaves no room for such phenomena as speakers who take part in election campaigns, street corner orators, luncheon-club circuit riders, salesmen approaching a succession of potential buyers, missionaries preaching in foreign societies, storefront information centers, literary agents, selective dissemination services and numerous others." He raises interesting research questions. For instance, "What sort of transactions, and, beyond these, what social processes are most likely to be fostered by each form of communication—*i.e.*, by mass communication and by each variety of quasi-mass communication. Which form is likely to lead to greater standardization and homogenization? Which is more nearly monopolizable by groups in power? Which offers the shelter of relative privacy to the transactions of novel, original, suppressed, minority, conspiratorial, or otherwise 'deviant' movements? Which will insulate interest groups from one another? And so on?"[19]

Global Issues

Let us move on to communication problems at the global level. Consider, first, the premise that the world is increasingly "informationized," this global "informationization" will figure in just about everybody's future, and the sooner and better we understand this phenomenon the greater our chance of finding ways to deal with it.

This tongue-twisting word "informationization" is used not to pervert the English language (it was coined in the 1960s by the Japanese as a translation of *johoka shakai*, meaning information society) but to stress a new importance of information in our lives. It suggests that information now plays an important role in social change today as steam power and electricity did in industrialization in the nineteenth century. Its meaning is broader than that of such words as "computerization,"[20] "compunication,"[21] and "teleinformatics."[22] It decribes not only a merger of computers and telecommunications but a fusion of various modes and systems of communication, an application of information to private and public affairs, and a process of development of information environments.

At any rate, the world is increasingly interconnected. It is "wired" quite differently now. The oldest nation-state in Europe is now a lot less national than before. Much of what European countries have to do these days depends on what kinds of arrangements they can work out with other countries. Development, the national policy of all developing countries, used to depend on national efforts. It now depends very heavily on international efforts. Increasingly, the issue is linked with a new agenda of global or cross-national welfare issues and policy problems—energy, ecology, health, population and poverty.

Rapid and continuing advances in communication and information technologies are changing not only the way the world communicates but also the way we perceive the world and ourselves. These technologies have restructured international relationships for many countries, redefined the world's political boundaries and economic resources, and reshaped the global balance of power.

Satellite technology, along with computer and microtechnology, is inherently international. It recognizes neither terrestrial boundaries nor political borders. It shrinks the world. It serves as a major factor in the integration of the developing countries into the world economic system, largely because of the reduced cost of satellite telecommunications. It has already affected the power relationships between governments and countries and is continuing to influence the reshaping and restructuring of traditional organizations and relations.

The world already is locked in a struggle for harnessing the communications and information technologies that represent the wave of the future. These technologies are a leading edge of U.S. strength. For the moment, the United States still dominates the field. Japan is scrambling to catch up, and many European industrialized countries are aggressively jockeying for position. Developing countries are seeking ways to reap the rewards of the new technologies, and some are trying to remake themselves through the technologies. While it is hard to take seriously the view that mastery of the microchip will allow poor countries to vault from underdevelopment into the computer society, it is easy to understand why these countries are determined to attempt some degree of mastery of the new information technology and not to miss out on the information revolution as some believe they did on the Industrial Revolution.

Information has acquired a quality of new strategic importance as a factor in international relations. Information is a much broader word than it was twenty years ago. It no longer refers only to conventional bodies of facts, figures, news, intelligence, or academic research. It includes all kinds of data ranging from electronic impulses that measure the human heartbeat to the signals in sensors that sight a target and guide a weapon to it.

Information also has become a new wealth of nations. More nations depend increasingly on information for the growth of the economy and for improvement of quality of life. The United States is now described as a country shifting from an industrial to an information economy.

This is not the place to argue whether the United States is an information society or whether the world is marching along a preindustrial–industrial–postindustrial path of development. What is important is that more and more industrial nations are devising plans and strategies to develop their information sectors—microchip technology, computers, and telecommunications.

What is even more important, but often overlooked, is the increasing interest and activity in communications development in the Third World and the desire to exploit new information technologies for developmental objectives — education, national integration, technololgy transfer, and health welfare services. A growing number of Third World countries have adopted national informatics plans and policies. Informatics, as defined by the Intergovernmental Bureau of Informatics, is the "rational and systematic application of information to economic, social and political development."

Yash Pol, secretary general of the Second United Nations Conference on Exploration and Peaceful Uses of Outer Space, reflected this mood of the Third World when he talked about satellite technology. "We can define neighborhoods in different terms from space," he said. "This provides us with a new agenda, a new perspective of what we should change, exploring the world of not only what is possible, but of what is desirable."[23]

Possession of information or data is not only a symbol of economic growth but a sign of power anywhere. Increasingly, a nation's political, economic, and military status in the world is defined or determined by its access to worldwide information and the possession of technology that collects and processes it.

There is no need to go into the implications of this phenomenon for international communication research. The possibilities for research are as plentiful as the problem is complex.

Broader Perspectives

Finally, a brief word about an entirely different problem. There was a time when mass communication research was identified by the media. We had newspaper research and radio research, an area distinguished by Lazarsfeld's work. Then much mass communication research was described and defined by the research methods that were used. Now the field is identified by the problems it studies.

What problems should be studied? This is a much harder question for academic communication researchers than for scientists. Physicists and chemists, for instance, generally know some of the toughest problems in the field, and the challenge is to find ways to crack them. Communication researchers do not always agree on the most important problems in the field. Their problems are also hard to master. Economist Gunnar Myrdal used to complain that social scientists "never reach down to constants like the speed of light and of sound in a particular medium, or the specific weights of atoms and molecules," that they "have nothing corresponding to the universally valid measurements of energy, voltage, amperes, and so on," and that the regularities they find do not have the "firm, general and lasting validity of a 'law of nature.'"[24] Mass communication researchers have to wrestle with more slippery problems than those in economics and on less firm ground.

The fact that mass communication researchers must work with scholars from various academic disciplines and professions makes the job of finding and defining problems even harder for them. Scholars in various disciplines have their own perspectives, and many are wedded to their ways to study a problem. Not many of them adapt very easily to a different perspective or a new set of terms.

Mass communication researchers cannot simply turn their problems to other scholars and leave the development of their field to the enterprise of others. They should alert scholars in various disciplines and professions to the critical issues in their field, and they must formulate questions for the consideration of other scholars. They must build bridges between their field and others. This is not to say that they cannot cross these bridges occasionally to get some ideas or borrow some tools from some disciplines. But not all the tools they need for research are necessarily available on the shelves of other disciplines; some perhaps do not even exist. Mass communication researchers must then know how to place special orders for these needed tools. For too long mass communication researchers have played a rather passive role with what a few fields of social science have to offer to the study of mass communication. And too many have seemed content to do their thing with the tools they have acquired from other fields.

Mass communication researchers have a far more important role to play than that. It would be asking too much to ask them to lead the study of mass communication in academic disciplines or to set a trend of mass communication research. But it is reasonable to expect them to at least do their part to set some of the future research agenda.

Notes

1. Ithiel de Sola Pool, "The New Structure of International Communication: The Role of Research," in International Association for Mass Communication Research, *New Structures of International Communication: The Role of Research* (Leicester, England: Adam Bros. & Shardlow Ltd., 1982), 61.

2. Ibid.

3. Wilbur Schramm, "The Unique Perspective of Communication, A Retrospective View," *Journal of Communication* 33 (Summer 1983): 12–13.

4. Ibid.

5. Jeremy Tunstall, "The Trouble with U.S. Communication Research," *Journal of Communication* 33 (Spring 1983): 92.

6. Berelson's idea was that the so-called "Founding Fathers" were leaving the field. He wrote that "Lasswell was interested in political power, Lewin in group functioning, and Hovland in cognitive processes, and they utilized this field (communication) as a convenient entry to these broader concerns." He said Lazarsfeld was the only one of the four who "centered on communication problems *per se*," but Lazarsfeld was then moving away into mathematical sociology. See Bernard Berelson, "The State of Communication Research," *Public Opinion Quarterly* 23 (Spring 1959): 1–6.

7. Herbert J. Gans, "The Famine in Mass Communication Research," *American Journal of Sociology* 77 (January 1972): 697–705.

8. Herbert J. Gans, "News Media, News Policy, and Democracy: Research for the Future," *Journal of Communication* 33 (Summer 1983): 174–84.

9. Wilbur Schramm, "Communication Research in the United States," in Wilbur Schramm, ed., *The Science of Human Communication* (New York: Basic Books, 1963), 2.

10. Wilbur Schramm, "The Unique Perspective of Communication," in his *Science of Human Communication*. Schramm is fond of using the parable about Bab elh-Dhra, a Bronze Age village, to illustrate what has been happening in the field of communication research. This village flourished some 5,000 years ago around an oasis just east of the Dead Sea. Schramm wrote:

> For centuries, Bab elh-Dhra, because it was noted for its good water, was a stopping place for caravans and travelers in the Jordanian desert. Then, shortly before 3,000 B.C., when farmers began to replace nomads, some families moved into Bab elh-Dhra and established a village. That settlement existed for a thousand years and passed out of human history. But it left its marks on walls and artifacts and tombs. . . . This is at least analogous to the kind of change that must have been underway when Berel-

son wrote his 1959 article. For many years, scholars, traveling with their own disciplinary maps, had stopped to look at communication problems, as travelers stopped to refresh themselves at the Jordanian oasis, and then moved on. . . . But a new type of scholar had already begun to appear in communication. This new scholar came to stay, not merely to visit.

11. Leo Bogart, "Consumer and Advertising Research," in Ithiel de Sola Pool, Wilbur Schramm et al., eds., *Handbook of Communication* (Chicago: Rand McNally, 1973), 706–21.

12. W. Phillips Davison and Frederick T. C. Yu, *Mass Communication Research: Major Issues and Future Directions* (New York: Praeger, 1974).

13. Herbert J. Gans, "News Media, News Policy, and Democracy," 174–84.

14. Ithiel de Sola Pool, "What Ferment?: A Challenge for Empirical Research," *Journal of Communication* 33 (Summer 1983): 258–61.

15. Edwin B. Parker, "Technological Change and the Mass Media," in Ithiel de Sola Pool, Wilbur Schramm, *et al., Handbook of Communication,* 639.

16. Edwin B. Parker, "Technology Assessment or Institutional Change?" in George Gerbner, Larry P. Gross, and William H. Melody, eds., *Communications Technology and Social Policy* (New York: John Wiley and Sons, 1973), 537.

17. Ithiel de Sola Pool, "The New Structure of International Communication: The Role of Research," in International Association for Mass Communication Research, *New Structures of International Communication,* 60–61.

18. Ibid., 63.

19. Herbert Menzel, "Quasi-Mass Communication: A Neglected Area," *Public Opinion Quarterly* 35 (Fall 1971): 406–9.

20. Simon Nora and Alain Minc, *The Computerization of Society: A Report to the President of France* (Cambridge: The MIT Press, 1981).

21. Coined by Anthony Oettinger of Harvard University's Program on Information Resources Policy.

22. John M. Eger, "The Global Phenomenon of Teleinformatics: An Introduction," *Cornell Information Law Journal* 14 (Summer 1981): 203–36.

23. Patrick Coolen, "LDC Reps Learn About Satcom at Hawaii Conference," *Satellite Communications* (March 1982): 62–63.

24. Gunnar Myrdal, *Against the Stream: Critical Essays on Economics* (New York, Pantheon Books, 1972), 138. See chapter on "How Scientific Are the Social Sciences?"

PART II

A Professional and Academic Dialogue

Having read the essays by Everette E. Dennis, David H. Weaver, and Frederick T. C. Yu, twenty leaders in communications research gathered at the S. I. Newhouse School of Public Communications for an open discussion.

Early in the proceedings the speakers tended to react to—and add to—what had been said in the papers, but soon the exchange of views took its own course. Perhaps the liveliest interchanges had to do with the cold war that was seen as characterizing the relationship between academics and professionals. Those in the opposing camps fired salvos at each other throughout much of the conference. The academics accused the professionals of making their research work futile by not supporting it, and worse, by ignoring it. The professionals charged the academics with not communicating research results in simple, understandable English. They particularly complained about what they saw as the arcane nature of research articles in academic journals.

In the end, however, a greater understanding of the needs and problems that existed on both sides was achieved. It was generally agreed that complete harmony between professionals and academics was probably not even advantageous; there were benefits to be reaped from some tension and separateness. However, the consensus was that professors and professionals need not be adversaries. Lines of communication should be kept open.

Challenges to Communications Research in the Age of Information

NANCY WEATHERLY SHARP

Understanding the role information plays in American society is essential to the preservation of freedom of speech in the country. And this will be even more crucial in a future that prognosticators have dubbed the "Age of Information" and have seen as becoming increasingly dominated by communications.

Nevertheless, despite notable exceptions, communications research has in the past—and continues in the present—to fall short. Although some excellent work has been done, those who study communications are too few and their work too often beset by one or more of a long list of difficulties. Many researchers—especially those from academia—lack adequate funding and are overburdened by other assignments. Some waste time on insignificant topics. Others, either as a result of secrecy amongst researchers working under contract for media organizations or the parochialism of academics, fail to build on the findings of other scholars. Most get little encouragement or attention for their work from communications practitioners or, for that matter, from anyone outside a small circle of research-oriented colleagues. Finally, the results of communications studies lead to few, if any, changes in the real world of the mass media.

The foregoing is the predominantly discouraging view of communications research that emerged from two days of candid, insightful, and often impassioned discussions among leading American communications experts who gathered at Syracuse University on December 6, 7, and 8, 1985, for the conference entitled "Communications Research: What, Why, and How?"

Participants struggled to pinpoint the character of communications research, to uncover its beginnings, to trace its evolution, and to see its future. A central question was: is communications research a discipline or field of study? By far the greatest amount of time was spent considering, measuring, and explaining the gap that all saw as separating academic researchers from

61

professionals in the communications world. Both Norman E. Isaacs, who has credentials as an editor as well as a university administrator, and J. Leonard Reinsch, chairman of Florida's Sunbelt Cable Ltd., referred to it as a "grand canyon." Initially most participants decried the estrangement. In the end, however, there seemed to be general agreement that certain differences were inevitable and probably healthy. Still, most participants continued to lament the degree of the alienation and looked for ways of mending fences. The conference-goers also worked hard to come up with ideas for invigorating the world of communications research and securing for it a more central role in the communications profession, the university, and society.

The Importance of Communications Research

Although most issues raised at the conference provoked spirited debate, on one question there seemed to be consensus—a consensus filled with urgency. Work of utmost importance, participants agreed, lay before communications researchers, and they must get on with it. It was critical to the future of American society, they said, for researchers to try to understand the various modes of communications, especially mass communications, that have become pervasive. There was also an avid interest in more practical research that could help practitioners make the mass media more successful, credible, and profitable.

In his essay Everette E. Dennis declared: "Knowing and understanding what mass communication can and cannot do has become a high stakes game." He called for "moving the research enterprise ahead" because "this is an information age when the needs of the citizens for understanding are high."

Frederick T. C. Yu made a similar assertion. "The world is increasingly 'informationized,' and the sooner and better we understand this phenomenon the greater our chance of finding ways to deal with it." He used the word *informationized* advisedly, he said, as the translation of a Japanese word meaning "information society." He likened the role of information in social change to that of steam power and electricity in the industrialization of the nineteenth century:

> Accelerating advances in the field of communication and information are changing not only the mass media but also the way we communicate, work, live, and organize our society. These developments and changes raise important questions about many of the ideas, methods, and institutions that have guided the study of mass communication during the past thirty to forty years.

They present exciting opportunities and pose enormous challenges for mass communication researchers.

Field or Discipline?

On another front sparks flew early in the conference proceedings. This was provoked by references in the conference papers to communications as both a field of study and also a discipline unto itself. Yu and Dean George Gerbner of the University of Pennsylvania emerged as the chief protagonists.

The discipline versus field of study dispute was first put before conference-goers in Dennis' paper: the difference between the two "is that in the former, mass communication is preeminent as a topic for study; in the latter, it is a sub-set of a scholar's primary discipline, whether politics, law, or social relations."

In supporting the view that communications was a field of study and, as such, required the work of scholars with many skills and representing many disciplines, Yu contested Wilbur Schramm's descriptions of communications research in 1963 as "an academic crossroad where many have passed but few have tarried" and twenty years later as "a new academic oasis." He said he found it "more fitting to think of mass communication research as a caravan on an intellectual expedition" than as a spot or region on an academic map. "This caravan has traveled some distance," Yu's analogy continued, "and traversed many crossroads. It is now *at* another crossroad. It has to know where it *is* going and where it *should be* going."

During the conference Yu took a bolder step. "When I was writing my paper," he explained, "I was thinking of another word. I was not courageous enough to put that word in. I will add it now. I think the field is not only in need of *rethinking* but perhaps even in need of *restructuring* in a way to get things done. I propose restructuring mainly because I am not in agreement with George Gerbner's idea about communication research as a discipline. I've al-ways been referring to it mainly as a field of study. I am not even sure that the idea of interdisciplinary is really quite the answer."

Perhaps, Yu suggested, trans-disciplinary was a better word than interdis-ciplinary: "You really have to have some bridges built and people go back and forth and do things. I would love to see a subsequent publication or conference sponsored by Syracuse University focus on rethinking this field—what to study and how to study it."

Gerbner took the opposite course, arguing vigorously: "Communications as a discipline reproduces the history of other disciplines as most of the disciplines now recognized in a traditional university have had fairly recent and relatively short histories, and all have stemmed from other disciplines."

Recalling the emergence of chemistry as a discipline, Gerbner contended that communications was at the stage that chemistry was at after having gone through the long period of alchemy:

> Alchemy was a very serious and very important undertaking. It was somewhat deluded in its quest for gold, and, in that, it perhaps also reproduced the history of the communications discipline. But changes in modern life required a broader approach involving chemical processes. Gold became only part of the game.
>
> Now, in communications most of the major contributions so far—and perhaps until maybe ten or fifteen years ago at least—have been made in the more traditional disciplines. We have now discovered for the past ten to twenty years that there are fundamental changes in the quality and the nature of our culture in regard to the making of messages surrounding human life. These have created a new situation whose basic dynamics have to be studied in a broad sense. Doing so requires taking full advantage of the contributions of other disciplines, but it makes a difference whether these pursuits are conducted within the framework of a communications program or of a sociology program or an anthropology program or really a radio-journalism advertising program.
>
> In each of these other disciplines communications processes, incidents, and developments are taken as cases in point to illuminate and test and develop theories about some other phenomenon, whether social structure or cultural processes. In communications these processes, incidents, and developments are seen within the framework of communications for institutional purposes. The basic objective is to develop and test theories of communication with the insights of sociology, of economics, of history. But, the emphasis is on how communication works rather than how social structure works and rather than how all of human behavior works.
>
> The basic task of a research program or graduate program in a discipline, then, is to build and test theories in that discipline, considering theories the most practical things in the world because they economize on practice and make it not only more economical but presumably more effective.

Not only did labeling communications a discipline make sense academically, Gerbner continued, it also made practical sense.

> Academic life is organized around disciplines so that in addition to the intellectual thrust on testing and developing theories, there is also the institutional pressure to define disciplines if you want to have legitimacy so that

you can compete with or against other disciplines for students or budgets. . . .

We consider a discipline an area of knowledge that has something to say about every human situation: economics, history, anthropology, psychology, sociology, etc. I believe that communications is such a discipline. It has to do with the nature and role of messages in society. It can contribute something to the understanding of any human situation. That understanding is unique to the human species because we are the only creatures who live in a world erected largely through messages and symbols. . . . We do not experience reality directly. Most of what is important to us here is really not in this room. It's in the realm of ideas. It's in the realm of the discourse to which we are transported through the messages that we exchange. And that is what the discipline is concerned with.

The discipline of communications could be divided into three interrelated components, Gerbner reasoned:

Put these three together and you have the structuring of a discipline in the way I find useful.

First is what we would call codes and modes. That has to do with the way of encoding, the way of structuring messages in languages in all their forms—verbal, nonverbal, gestural, etc. Just how do we produce large systems of messages?

Second is what happens as we exchange these messages. What characteristics do we as communicating parties provide and attribute to the messages? What have our own personal, social, and other roles to do with the way in which we interpret and use messages?

The third is concerned with large systems and institutions, such as the mass media, such as the communication component of any organizational life. And that deals with the history, the management, the decision-making processes in large institutions.

The process of communication, Gerbner said, has developed in three stages:

The pre-industrial form of communication was all face-to-face, ritualized, encompassing the whole tribe or community. Then came print, the first industrial revolution in the way we constructed messages. Most of our assumptions about government, social life, education, religion, and so on, stem from the print era. Print broke up the ritual. It broke up the rule of the priestly caste over the communication of stories about life. It made pluralistic life possible. It made the rise of modern mass publics possible. Mass publics are people who share a great deal in common but never see each other face to face. Now the third era we're in is the telecommunications era whose flagship is television and which has one unique characteristic: it's a ritual. Most people watch by the clock and not by the program. It has more to do with tribal religion than with print. And it is used relatively non-selectively. All other media are used selectively, which I consider to be the crucial distinction. Selectively used media require literacy, require mobility, require a development of tastes, ideas, and attitudes that lead to the selection. A non-selectively used medium is one into which children are inserted at birth. They absorb many of their patterns before they ever become literate, before they ever start moving around. The medium shapes their preconceptions. The new technologies of communications can then be sorted out as to whether they are more likely to enhance the diversity of selection or whether they extend the relatively non-selective use of pre-programmed information and entertainment.

Leo Bogart entered the discussion to question whether communications was, in fact, a discipline. Did it "really represent a cohesive body of knowledge that deserves the creation of a special tribe of dedicated scholars?" asked the executive vice president of the Newspaper Advertising Bureau.

Bogart said he was educated at a time when sociology was taught in government departments. "There was no political science as distinct from government or sociology," he recalled. "I studied psychology in a department of philosophy and psychology. We've seen the slow and painful emergence of separate disciplines in most universities in those areas. I just wonder if communications is ready to stand up and declare itself a discipline in the same essential sense that sociology, economics, psychology, and anthropology have."

Research Falling Short

Although conference participants saw scholarly investigations of communications as of paramount importance, they agreed that to date the yield had been disappointing. Mass communications researchers, they said, had not come to grips with the central issues of communications in American society.

All three paper writers emphasized this. Dennis lamented that "while there is communication research of the highest quality . . . it is also true that the overall quality is not impressive." Yu said that mass communication research lacked direction, was not as intellectual, exciting, or socially useful as it should be, and did not command respect either in the academic world or the communications profession.

I just feel that in studying the major question—what kind of a system do we have, to what extent and in what way is it meeting the needs of society, and to what extent and in what way might it meet those needs a little better—we make a number of assumptions. We really don't even know those needs. We haven't even made many important studies of those needs. We have assumptions.

David H. Weaver talked about a lack of "substance." First on his list of problems with communications research was "a lack of application to important social and scholarly issues." Faulting communications scholars for being sidetracked by "trivial research," he claimed that too much research had "little relationship to broad general theories of society and social trends and to important social values."

Weaver's complaints provoked a rebuttal from Gerbner, who warned against quickly categorizing research as lacking significance:

What may be trivial from one point of view may be extremely important from another. Research is really an artistic act. Research is a question of imagination. I would be very cautious in getting any kind of a general rule as to what is trivial research.

When research is done out of ignorance of what has been done, it's a waste of time. But the history of science is full of examples of serendipitous research whose significance was not seen at the time—except perhaps by the investigator—that became important for some subsequent discovery or subsequent follow-up. So, I would say that any research that attempts to extend or challenge an existing theory in the field, no matter how modest (and modesty is usually a question of budget), is non-trivial.

Research that is representative, that is only replicated, that is only doing something because this is done in the field—and our students are full of those ideas, you know, until they put up enough resistance to challenge their imaginations—I would consider of less importance. But anything that is fresh, imaginative, original, and attempts, even in a modest way, to challenge or extend a basic assumption—even if the findings are negative, even if it fails—I would say is non-trivial.

Gerbner then related his comments to Weaver's paper, which, he said, categorized some of his own research as trivia:

In his paper Weaver says that an example of trivial research is the finding that 11.4 percent of the characters in soap operas are mentally ill. We have done some of that research, and I happen to think that it's a very significant finding, not in itself but in its implications and its uses. . . . It so happens that the portrayal of that 11.4 percent is the single major source of ideas about emotional and mental illness for the general public. And it is the nature of that portrayal that conditions the way in which we relate to people who are labeled or diagnosed as having some kind of mental problem.

Our research on that was commissioned by the National Institute of Mental Health, which is in the business of finding out about the influences that condition the treatment of the mentally ill. We have been invited to many of their meetings to communicate precisely that kind of an image, and so we have developed a fairly comprehensive view of the different cultural influences that in turn become problems for the therapists and problems for people who are placed into certain roles if they are labeled ex-mental patients or mentally ill or something like that.

Weaver assured Gerbner that his work was not the target of his criticism. "It was another study whose researchers didn't do what you did," he said. "They didn't go beyond the percentage of soap opera time devoted to mental illness. I think I singled that out because that was one of the major findings of the study just in isolation by itself, and it wasn't reported in your journal [*Journal of Communication*]."

Weaver added that he agreed with what Gerbner had said: "My conception of trivial research is research that doesn't seem to have any connection with the basic assumptions or theories in our field or doesn't seem to have any context to it. It seems to be an exercise in doing something for the sake of getting a study."

Questions for Researchers

In critiquing topics that had been investigated by communications scholars to date, Dennis pointed to the work that had been done on media power—the impact, influence, and effect of mass communications—and to recent work on media ethics as areas of strength. However, he found questions surrounding freedom of expression, economics (including ownership patterns of the media), and technology to have been inadequately dealt with. There was only a limited literature tracing the information revolution and the emergence of the information society, he said.

Other conference-goers called for more studies on freedom of information issues as well as for analyses of the internal structure and workings of the U.S. media system and its social impact on society.

"We fight for a free press in the interest of a free society," Isaacs said with some feeling, "because without that underpinning of free communication a free society cannot survive. At the bottom of all of this has to come a solid research foundation." Isaacs cited challenges to freedom of expression stemming from public attitudes toward the media and resulting in a chilling of media activities as "profound reasons to be involved, profound reasons for mutual respect between the practitioner and the scholar."

Shirley Wilkins, president of The Roper Organization, concurred: "The freedom of press issues are enormous. Our studies show that news people *per se* and the press and television people now have a great wellspring of good will upon which to draw. But there are problems with public perceptions. These are things that need to be addressed. We have got to keep that good will alive to keep our society alive."

Frank Stanton, president emeritus of CBS, Inc., was among the conference participants who saw value in studying the inner workings of the media and evaluating the degree to which these media were meeting the needs of the society. He predicted a shift toward news storytelling in the next ten years, in part as a result of new media distribution patterns:

Look at the networks today. They don't produce their own entertainment programs. Those are all from the outside. All a network is is a mechanism to distribute. You don't need that mechanism if you really want to get down to the nitty-gritty because technology will allow you to transmit directly to the stations from Hollywood without ever coming through a network.

Now, with all the independent opportunities for producing broadcasts in the news area, you could distribute them the same way—without a network. So what does the network have? It has really a very efficient selling mechanism, perhaps an efficient promotion organization. But it doesn't have a more efficient distribution system than you can get by any other means, particularly by cable or by satellite.

In order for network news to survive in this marketplace it's going to have to shift much more into the storytelling mode. And it's going to be— I abhor it, but that's my age—given with much more simplicity, and it's going to be much more like the "Entertainment Tonight" television show than it is like the news in what some of you might call the golden age of television news. It's a fundamental issue that has to be faced by the industry owner and by the academic world as well.

Stanton pointed to management changes at CBS as evidence, especially the elevation of Van Gordon Sauter several days before the conference to the presidency of CBS News. "The role model for Sauter," Stanton said, "is 'Entertainment Tonight.' He was the one who picked Phyllis George, I am told. He took her out of the world of Miss America and sports to have her do the 'Morning News,' and that's an enormous change as far as the distribution of the news is concerned. And, like it or not, that shift is now taking place. It has taken place."[1]

Bogart raised two issues for researchers. The first was the new electronic technology and its implications for changing the structure of the media and the consumption of information and entertainment by the public. The second, echoing a concern of Dennis', had to do with media ownership. What effect, Bogart asked, would the increasing concentration of ownership, the increasing emphasis on acquisition and agglomeration, have on an industry that historically had been characterized by a great deal of local autonomy and independence?

Chain and conglomerate ownership also interested Isaacs:

> Some of us have come to know the qualitative nature of certain chains as against others. I myself am given to broad statement about journalistic stinkers. There is no real body of research that I know of that has been done about qualitative content or attitudes of chains. I can name certain chains for which I have some admiration. I think the Knight-Ridder organization has distinguished itself by and large in print on the remarkable degree of autonomy it has granted its publishers and editors. I think to a large extent for some years this has been true of the Times Mirror Corporation, which publishes the Los Angeles *Times*. I think Katharine Graham has won a good deal of applause for her handling of the *Post-Newsweek* stations. . . . But we really have no basis of fact; nobody has done any deep research on this. We don't know what the relationships are to earnings, and the earnings are perfectly possible to get because these are public corporations. No studies have been made within communities about what the community attitudes are about these news organizations.

Bogart's suggestion that researchers look into the implications of media technology prompted a response from Gerbner, who asserted that technology had changed the way people were informed and even socialized, and this should change the way researchers gathered their information:

> Because of new technological developments, starting with television and then accelerating ever since, the concept of information has been transformed and is becoming something quite different from the classical traditional concept that saw what we call information—information about government, about

occupations, about health, about religions, information about society—as coming mostly from news, the press. This simply no longer holds true.

Social information for most people today comes primarily from what we call entertainment. Audiences are plunged into a world of stories largely, but not exclusively, because of the influence of television from infancy, where, during the first six years of life and after, the basic social information comes from all of the stories people are being told. . . .

The course of information has changed and every medium has to adjust and adapt to that new climate. But this does not neatly connect with the existing organization of the industry. It doesn't neatly connect with the existing compartmentalization of information and education, entertainment, persuasion, all of which have lost their basic meanings. We have to think about storytelling in a new way.

Later in the proceedings, Gerbner posed a question (that he labeled unpopular) for researchers. It went beyond studying the existing media system:

Is the structure of the system itself one that can be adjusted, that can be improved, that can be reviewed? This is a question that inevitably leads somebody to lose money and perhaps no clearly identifiable party to gain. It is an impractical question from the media practitioner point of view, but it is a question that is essential in the long run for the survival of a free society.

Gerbner concluded by suggesting that research in the developing discipline of communications had three objectives:

First of all it should provide information for the industry, for citizens, for legislators.

The second major task is to contribute a fresh approach to the liberal arts. The liberal arts are the liberating arts. Historically, they were used to liberate individuals from their parochial environments and put them in touch with the great philosophies of humankind. Today, there is no such parochial environment. We are living in an information-rich, mechanized, mass-produced society and what we have to be liberated from is an unquestioning acceptance of the assumptions on which it rests. Looking analytically and critically at our everyday cultural environment is the contribution that communications research can make to the academy, to undergraduate education, to high schools, and to education at every level.

Lastly, I think the third contribution of communications research should be to provide the raw materials for a new environmental movement—a movement that is as concerned with improving the quality and nature of the symbolic environment (which is largely mass-produced today) as some are today with the physical environment. It will require a major social investment, and in order to determine where that investment might be the least harmful and the most useful, ammunition will be needed in the form of information that communications research can provide.

This third area, Gerbner said, was increasingly becoming of interest to citizens and community groups, such as Action for Children's Television.

Louis Boccardi, president of the Associated Press, quickly posed a question to Gerbner. "Are there any dangers to free expression in that third step?" he asked. "Could it lead to a kind of one-issue vigilantism?"

"There are great dangers in any free expression," Gerbner replied, adding that freedom of the press could lead to the publication of irresponsible statements and academic freedom could lead to irresponsible statements coming out of the academy. "We just have to live dangerously."

The Grand Canyon

The question of issues for researchers to investigate, like most of the subjects at the conference, revealed the differences and suspicions that separated the academicians from the practitioners and sparked quarrels between the two. Those in the former group tended to view those in the latter as not all that serious about issues of substance but only concerned with how research results could affect their balance sheets. At the same time, the practitioners found fault with the academics, charging that their work was often obscure and crammed with incomprehensible statistical material. It was no wonder, they said, that academic research rarely captured the attention of media professionals and provoked few changes in the communications world.

Research Topics

Daniel B. Wackman, from the School of Journalism and Mass Communication at the University of Minnesota, tried to differentiate communications from other professional fields. Although he saluted the *Harvard Business Review* as an excellent mechanism for bringing research news to a comparatively broad audience, he cautioned against those in the communications field following in the footsteps of their colleagues in management and business:

Research in management and business is not a very good model for us in the sense that I don't see much research there about the role of business and its impact on society, which is what a great body of the mass communication researchers are interested in. They don't do that sort of thing. We *do* do that sort of thing, and that's a major purpose of people in journalism schools and their research. And too often there does not appear to be any legitimization by industry of that kind of activity.

Wackman tried to open a dialogue by putting questions to the practitioners on the conference podium, saying he would like to see some mechanism established for identifying social questions that industry leaders found important:

What social impacts are you interested in having research done about? What aspects of the structure of your organizations would you like to know something about? Those are the *what* kinds of questions that I think are almost a necessary starting point. I'm not sure that the *whats* that people in the media industry have in mind are the same as the *whats* the academic communities have in mind.

Kristin McGrath, president of Minnesota Opinion Research, Boccardi, and Reinsch each spoke for the practitioners.

Boccardi mentioned topics of interest to him personally, which he agreed to put forward "just off the top of my head":

The first has to do with young adults, where they are getting their information and why we seem to have such a problem with them and newspaper reading. We pride ourselves on Americans being so well informed by an information system that is magnificent in comparison with those in the rest of the world. I saw a piece of research the other day, though, that said half of the citizens of this country can't name their congressmen. Before we congratulate ourselves too much, we ought to look at some of the problems. So, the question of how Americans obtain their information and what they do with it is another issue. The fact that editors or news organizations have invested substantial sums in two major studies of the public perception of the press would suggest to you that that's yet another area of interest.

Research questions having to do with radio also were brought up by Boccardi. "Radio stations are changing hands at a tremendous clip," he said. "What does that mean, if anything? What impact has there been on radio news in relation to the fact that the FCC environment has changed so much. What about the phenomenon of radio stations just abandoning news in a lot of cases?

"These would be some examples of research areas that it would seem to me to have an academic, a societal point, but also at some stage in the research a good deal of utility."

Wackman asked Boccardi if impacts on audiences, on society, on differentiation and knowledge levels in society, interested him. Boccardi replied:

> Yes, but I think my interest begins a little more parochially than that. And it seems to me it wouldn't be unnatural for your interest to be more global and that the real work will get done somewhere in the middle. The things I have talked about obviously have an immediate and useful kind of connotation. As a newspaper person or as a broadcast newsman one has an interest in what is happening in radio news or why young people are not reading newspapers. There are some societal points to be taken out of all that. And I don't think the professional would be against some lessons to be derived. We won't turn away from a piece of research because you try to make it somewhat more substantial. It would help us understand the narrow point, the point where we try to apply what you do. The better informed we are when we get to that point with the broader background that you could give us certainly would help us make better decisions when at some end point we put our own editorial intuition into what you develop.

McGrath said that people in the communications industry were not interested only in studies with direct applications. "In my work with a lot of newspapers," she said, "I have run into a lot of very thoughtful people who are interested in both useful issues and also worthwhile and important ones, people not looking primarily at 'quick-fix' kinds of things. The editors I have run into are looking very much long term."

Reinsch said it was only appropriate that practitioners and researchers looked at the field from different perspectives:

> I think we have two different fields here. Some of the research that's done in the academic field does not necessarily have to be accepted or applied in the business field. It may serve a new purpose in general society. I think that in business we have to consider the bottom line. Otherwise, we're out of work. People in the academic field have to understand that those of us who are in the electronic media—I don't want to speak for the print media—do have some fundamental constraints.

It was in 1934, Reinsch said, that he had been introduced to survey research and he had been interested in the subject ever since:

I think that we have been using much of the material. It may not always be evident. We are interested in the social implications of what we are doing. I'm particularly concerned and interested in the increasing impact of cable. And there is probably no research in this field today. Our experience in the field shows that cable is having a very powerful impact on viewing habits, on people's opinions, and even on their living habits. We are not unmindful of what you in academic research are doing. Sometimes I think you're not always mindful of what we're doing.

David Rubin, chairman of the Department of Journalism and Mass Communication at New York University, brought up his study on arms control coverage as a case in point for media professionals to consider. "It's a research effort," he explained, "to look at how the press covers the arms race. And the ultimate purpose is to try to shed some light on what questions are looked at, what questions are ignored, and to what depth the press goes with what sort of consistency."

Addressing the media professionals at the conference, Rubin asked if they wanted to know what he was doing and what he found out. "What would you do with our findings if you got them?" he asked. "Do you think the question is worth studying?"

Edward R. Cony, vice president/news for Dow Jones, publisher of the *Wall Street Journal* and the Ottaway Newspapers, and Boccardi were quick to respond. Boccardi said:

If you did such a study, I would read it. I would be interested in the findings and would want to know something about how you got where you got. There is a problem sometimes with studies that start with a point of view, and one of the things I look at when I look at a study is whether that clouds the nature of the findings.

I think that as a practitioner I need to take whatever you find and try to put it into the framework I have, which is one of meeting with what we perceive to be the news needs of the editors and broadcasters we serve. So, finding that there isn't as much coverage of the arms race as your research group thinks there should be might not be instructive. It might be instructive if it showed that certain aspects of the arms race were covered to the detriment of others or covered in ways that didn't fit the truth of the issue as you find it—not that we would have lied but that our emphasis might not have given a broader, more accurate picture.

Cony wondered how researchers expected practitioners to react to their findings:

Certainly there is no issue facing mankind that is more serious than the arms race, and I don't think anybody in this room would argue that it doesn't need to be covered in depth and with understanding. I would like to see what you have to say, but Lou Boccardi has touched on one thing that I think is almost universal. That is that almost any project by any group will find there to be less press coverage than the group would like the subject studied to have. We almost never get a complaint about too much coverage. And that can lead to skepticism among professionals about the value of research.

Boccardi carried the argument one step further:

I think for those of us responsible for creating news as a product there is an intelligent way to use research. But leadership—the intuitive sense of the editor or the news director or the broadcaster as to what a product should be—is something that doesn't come only from research. In other words, I think that the best of what researchers do takes you to a point. But there is a point where leadership has to take over. That sense in the heart of the editor or the broadcaster of what a story should be and what his or her newspaper should do for the community is something that is better informed by what researchers can do. But I don't know many good editors who are willing to let research edit their papers.

Bogart agreed. "How much time or space you devote to nuclear issues or arms control issues is a policy matter that is not amenable to research as such. It's a question of will. It's a question of morality. It's a question of judgment."

An editor can be independent and sensitive to issues at the same time, Isaacs added:

I am conscious of the space and time issue, but at least for one stretch of my life I lived in a charmed world where the importance of an issue took precedence over the bottom line. In other words, in response to a nuclear issue, if it had arisen at that time, I would not have hesitated to have taken pages and pages, day after day, to harp home the basic issues, to give the readers all the information I could so that they could see the importance of it. As long as we were making a profit anyway, my concern was with the quality of service.

We have a few newspapers in the United States that way now. For instance, you look at the New York *Times*, and you will see an investment of space in stories of major importance. The Los Angeles *Times* is another. The Washington *Post* is still another.

Reinsch applied what Cony and Isaacs said to the electronic media, predicting that Rubin's research project would conclude that there was not enough television news coverage of the arms race:

> The general reaction is going to be that we don't do enough. Well, we have the constraints of time. The nuclear issue is not going to be conveyed to the public in one week, two weeks, a month, two months, or even a year. While you have plenty of newsprint to put into a discussion, television is, after all, the popular way of conveying information. We have an obligation to present all the news, and, if we take twenty of the twenty-two minutes to describe the nuclear issue, we are lost. Now we have to make separate programs. We can have a Sunday program. We can have a discussion program. But this is a subject that is complex. Readers or viewers are not going to be educated about it in a short period of time.

Mark Levy, associate professor at the College of Journalism, University of Maryland, answered the professionals. "What you have said," he argued, "reminds me so much of what I constantly run up against when I do consulting with practitioners who answer any complaints that there is not enough about arms control with 'Oh, we don't have enough time.' That's not where the discussion should end. It's where it should begin. Why isn't there enough time? What is there about the product that might be changed?"

"But the discussion has to go beyond that," Reinsch responded, "if we are going to give more time to arms control. We have to eliminate something else. Are we eliminating the right subjects when we eliminate the material to provide the time?"

Levy suggested that the larger question was how well broadcasters were communicating in their twenty-two-minute news holes in the first place. "I have raised that question with NBC News and independent television, with the BBC, and my colleagues with television in Israel and elsewhere around the world. And time after time the professional journalist says, 'You're intruding on our autonomy. Buzz off. We don't want to hear about it.'"

Rubin picked up on the issue of quality. "I find it interesting," he said, "that both Mr. Reinsch and Ed Cony discussed the issue of the quantity of the coverage of the arms race. As somebody who has just spent the last two or three weeks watching the summit coverage and reading about the summit, I would say that the last thing you have to worry about is *quantity* of coverage.[2] There was certainly enough time and space devoted to the summit. We brought home from Geneva the entire Associated Press file, and it filled one entire suitcase. The fact that you all settled on the quantity of coverage as the issue to raise first—at least it popped into your minds first—may tell me something, however, about the gap between you there and me here."

Rubin sought feedback on two research questions growing out of the summit that he found intriguing:

> One, there has been a lot of research on reporter-source relationships in an American context. *Journalism Quarterly* and other journals have been filled with it. Let's assume for the moment that representatives of the Soviet Union continue to be as outspoken and as freely available to the Western press as they were in Geneva. Let's assume that this continues not just at extraordinary meetings like the summit but even in Moscow. Now, for me, that raises some very interesting questions about the reporter-source relationship. When the reporter is a Western reporter, reporting for a Western audience, and the source is a Soviet citizen, diplomat, or whatever, I think the rules of the game will be completely different for lots of reasons. I think that's worth looking at. I hope it interests you.
>
> A second one is this. I am a great believer in the fact that the people in the business make a difference. I wouldn't be in journalism education if I wasn't. I don't believe that reporters are spark plugs and that you can put one in and take one out and the paper rolls on with the same quality of coverage. I think the quality is very much dependent on the people you hire to do the job. As a result I am interested in doing profiles of the people who cover the arms race, looking at their world views and what they see as the appropriate place of the United States in the world. I think that approaching the quality of coverage from that perspective is different. It interests me, but, if it doesn't interest the professional side, that's where you get discussions of gaps, miscommunication. Journalists are uncomfortable talking about such things. Many say they have no opinions on such matters, even journalists who cover national security questions. I don't believe that.

Boccardi answered, first by cautioning Rubin about expecting the Soviets to emulate Western standards of press openness:

> It's one thing to put a spokesman in a room with lights that blind the speaker. It's quite another to permit the press to operate in anything like the Western model. So, I hope you would not equate some press conferencing, should it start, with the Western approach to the press.
>
> On your second point about what the reporters believe, you're right in introducing that as a difficult and sensitive question. I would assert to you that nobody in my company knows my political views. And I know the political views of very few people in the AP. I think that's quite healthy and I certainly don't want to read their political views in your research paper.

No one has established to my satisfaction—maybe your researchers have done it and I haven't read it—that the personal point of view of the reporter does, in fact, impact the coverage.

There was a fuss made a few years ago about the finding that the beliefs of reporters were more liberal than those in society generally, but nobody I know of has taken it the next step and established that it really makes any difference anyway. So, I am uncomfortable with the idea that what the reporter believes about President Reagan's competence as president is germane to whether he or she can cover him fairly. I would like to look at the coverage and not at the reporter's personal beliefs.

Rubin asked if there weren't a link between the two. A reply came from Gerbner. "We have done a study," he said, "that supports the view that what comes out—and even more importantly what is remembered or what is acted upon or responded to—does not reflect the personal view of the individual reporter. It does, however, reflect the total ideological position of the institution in which the reporter works, which is a different matter."

The lengthy discussion about research topics exasperated Levy, who virtually threw up his hands. Many of the topics suggested by practitioners as interesting ones to look into, he claimed, had already been investigated by himself and other academicians:

I have been sitting here for the better part of the day now, and I am getting more and more frustrated with what I consider to be the level of 'Before Syracuse.' I think the victim in all of this is the academic researcher.

The findings are available. Some of the work I.have done personally and have tried to share with my colleagues in the profession with no success. So, I am really, I must confess, on balance feeling like we're talking past each other. I think, if anything, it's like the recent summit, where both countries came, said their pieces, and suggested that maybe the sides ought to talk again.

The practitioners defended themselves. In direct response to Levy, Boccardi said he knew that the issues he had mentioned were not new. "They are enduring issues," he said, "and issues that, it seems to me, would be of some research value. I was responding to a question about what problems we are trying to solve. It was in that context that I answered."

Levy pressed him: "But if they are serious problems to you, you should have been going to the people who have done the work on them. I think if you had done that you would have found that there is research that is interesting to you, that is valuable to you, that may actually be troubling to you because it may cause you to reflect on some cherished professional beliefs and values, which may, in fact, be completely wrong-headed."

Sharing Information

The exchange of views caused Isaacs to ask if there were some central bank of information that news organization research departments could tap to get at research results.

"There used to be," Philip Meyer, the William Rand Kenan, Jr., Professor of Journalism at the University of North Carolina, responded. "The American Newspaper Publishers Association used to have one but they cut off its funding in budget cutbacks."

Even though there no longer was a central bank, Dennis argued that it was relatively easy for practitioners to get their hands on data. "There is an enormous amount of networking in this country," he pointed out. "I get calls almost every day from people at news organizations asking if I know where to find information about such and such. And I tell them that somebody at the University of Somewhere is doing something on that and why don't they give that person a call."

Rubin continued:

> If Lou Boccardi is interested in this sort of stuff he can consult with anyone in this room as to the dozen or so journals that would be best for the AP to subscribe to. It would also be possible to have somebody on the AP staff, called research director, organize and categorize and be prepared to brief Lou when he needed to know if X or Y existed. If that were too complicated, there are people like Mark Levy who would be happy to be a consultant to AP.

Like Dennis, Rubin said, he was often contacted by practitioners but sometimes found the calls discouraging:

> I frequently get calls from media people who want to know if anything has been done in certain areas. First, let me say, I appreciate the calls and I do what I can to point people in different directions. But I frequently get calls from television people who want to know whether there have been studies done on the portrayal of certain groups on television, such as the elderly. When I mention Dean Gerbner to them, they have never even heard of him. No one in the industry, particularly in television, can be serious about re-

search dealing with television and not know who he is. It means to me that
there is no real interest except in the chaotic deadline sense, which is the way
journalism works.

At least communication did go on, Bogart pointed out, between academics and commercial researchers like himself. "We depend both on academic
journals and on our colleagues in academia," he said.

The practitioners kept insisting, and somewhat heatedly, that they would
be less estranged from academic researchers if only those researchers would
write—*Journalism Quarterly* came in for its share of criticism—in plain English.
The researchers rejoined by saying that the statistical portions of their studies
needed to be published so that other researchers could evaluate their methods
and replicate their work. Furthermore, they argued, if the practitioners were
really interested in research, they would learn how to read and evaluate it.

"The reaction of most of the people I talk to," Isaacs said, "is that if *Journalism Quarterly* is the mirror through which the research capacity of academic
journalism shows what it's got, then God help us because damn few of us can
understand it." He would love to read *Journalism Quarterly*, he quipped sar-
castically but good naturedly, "but my education isn't that far advanced."

"It's not fair for me to say anything about *Journalism Quarterly*," Boccardi
said, "because I haven't looked at it in a decade, certainly more":

> But I know what my reaction was when I did look at it. I found it impene-
> trable. Unless you who are doing this research and are in a position to con-
> tribute to the busy people on the other side can find a way to communicate
> your findings more effectively than you have, you can have a conference
> like this every five years and the text is going to turn out sort of the same.
> There are lots of questions in the news rooms of America. And you could
> help with them, but your research needs to be reported in a way that we
> can understand without going out and hiring somebody to translate for us.
> I think that undermines the process.

Cony also found research articles difficult reading:

> It's not the kind of writing that we do in our business because we have to
> be conscious—and everybody should be—that you can't force anybody to
> read anything. You have to tempt readers. And that's why there is so much
> concern about the quality of writing in newspapers and magazines. We can
> sit here all day, and I can tell you that you should read my newspaper. But
> if I'm not presenting stuff that interests you, you're not going to read it. So

much depends on language, and I think in general that the language in communications research is stilted and not very interesting.

Several conference participants, however, said that the reason academic journals were not read by the practitioners was more basic and substantive than the language problem. The real question, Yu said, was whether academic research had enough of importance to say to people in the communications industry: "This concerns subjects of study rather than the method of presentation or the language that's used to communicate the findings."

Weaver explained the need for some of the language that frustrated the professionals. "Academic researchers have to talk to each other in a specific language to tell each other how they have conducted their studies so the studies can be replicated," he said. "It's difficult for a journal to satisfy both scholars and people out working in journalism and mass communication."

Other professional fields, Weaver claimed, didn't have the same problem. "Lawyers can talk to each other, whether they're in the university doing research or whether they're outside practicing," he said. "It's the same with doctors. They can read medical journals and understand what the authors are saying." In line with this, both Stanton and Bogart suggested that perhaps professors of communications courses should prepare their students to read communications research articles intelligently.

Yu likened the language used by communications researchers to jargon:

It's easy to be critical of *Journalism Quarterly* so far as the quality of writing is concerned. However, I'm not sure whether the important question is really that it has esoteric language or too much jargon. I think jargon is available in almost every field, even in newspapers. To this day I don't read all the sports pages because some of the articles I don't understand. I have never bothered to learn the jargon.

On the other hand, to be very blunt about it, if a group wants to know what is going on in a field, even if the language is difficult, I think efforts are made to understand it. In almost every field there is a point at which you really have to have background information to understand what is being said.

However, if research articles were unnecessarily difficult to read, Yu said, it was regrettable: "When medical doctors don't write well, they get away with it. But when communication researchers do not write clearly, I think they're justifiably, understandably blamed." Some communications research journals, however, Yu said, were more readable than others, singling out the *Columbia Journalism Review* and the *Journal of Communication*.

Gerbner denied that the language in the journals was all that formidable: "I submit that most of the material is nontechnical, nonspecialized, and perfectly readable. Some is more difficult, but the difficulty in reading any of it has more to do with motivation than with the actual difficulty of language."

Media professionals could inform themselves about academic research by reading journal articles selectively, Weaver said:

People who aren't trained in quantitative methodology shouldn't find it surprising that they cannot read and interpret the tables and the statistical data in some *Journalism Quarterly* articles. But they can read the introductions. They can read the summaries and conclusions even if they don't have a shred of knowledge about quantitative methods. And they can ask, "Does this tell me anything about journalism or mass communication that I didn't know before?"

Bogart continued:

If you look at the articles in *Journalism Quarterly* and other scholarly publications that are full of statistical tables—and *Journalism Quarterly* is far less impenetrable than most journals in the social sciences—you will always find at the end either a statement calling for more research or supporting or disproving the opening hypothesis. So, you do learn what the bottom line is.

Arnold H. Ismach advised news organizations to hire people to translate and interpret journal articles because they contained worthwhile research findings that had implications for the news business. He regretted that *Journalism Quarterly* was not found in most news rooms. "When it is there," he said, "it's not read. The issues stay on the shelves, untouched. News people forever tell you that they're word people, not number people. They don't want to be confused with statistics."

Meyer urged the professional communicators on both sides of the communications research gap to use their skills. "If the Associated Press decided it wasn't going to cover medical stories because the articles in the *New England Journal of Medicine* were too hard to read, it wouldn't be anywhere," he pointed out. The communications problem could be solved by a professional translator who would summarize research findings for practitioners in some kind of newsletter format, he said. Weaver brought up one such effort at bridging the gap, the "News Research" column written by Guido H. Stempel III, editor of *Journalism Quarterly* and distinguished professor of journalism at the E. W. Scripps School of Journalism at Ohio University, for *presstime*, the journal of the American Newspaper Publishers Association (ANPA).

Gerbner said the interest of communications practitioners in research depended on their goals:

> The problem is that the communications industry has never—perhaps for good historical reasons—made up its mind as to what it wants to do besides make money. Now if you're making snake oil, you don't need to know the literature. All you need to know is what makes the product sell. I'm not saying that the communications business is comparable to making snake oil, but it is comparable in that sense. As long as the bottom line is the primary determinant, you have an essentially pragmatic and empirical test at the box office, and you don't need much research.

Even in the communications field, practitioners, could read statistics in instances where money was involved, Gerbner said. The A. C. Nielsen Co. did research in audience measurement, he said, and:

> I haven't heard broadcasters complain that they cannot read those statistics. The Audit Bureau of Circulations publishes [readership] research, and I haven't heard publishers say they cannot read those complicated tables. When it comes down to bread and butter, they can prepare, they can read, they can use.
>
> If you have other objectives, if you want to know what happens when your messages touch the lives of people—whether they buy or not—if you want to know how your chemistry interacts when it is taken in and given out by living people, how it shapes their conceptions of life and of themselves, you enter a much more technical, a much more difficult and highly complex area. Then you have the motivation to learn the specialized languages that are most effective for communicating that information.

McGrath had an explanation for why communications professionals—at least those working for newspapers—were more familiar with the bread-and-butter type studies Gerbner cited. It revealed another dimension of the communications gap:

> The organization of newspapers as regards research may be one reason for the gap we have been talking about. Although there are a few exceptions

right here in this room, the researchers at newspapers tend not to have come from journalism schools or communications research programs. These people —and you will see this if you attend a meeting of the Newspaper Research Council[3]—have come from business schools. So one question to ask is why these people are coming from a business/marketing background in which they have not been exposed to the kinds of issues we have been talking about. They really can't talk—and don't—to communications researchers. So, it might help us to look at the organization of the media as well as the organization of academia.

Both Meyer and Isaacs responded to McGrath's statement, the first by describing the Newspaper Research Council as a particularly insular organization, an organization not receptive to academics. Isaacs observed that a number of newspaper organizations had recently advanced journalists, rather than business people, to top executive positions and predicted that this might change the type of individuals who were funneled into the research side of the enterprise. "It used to be," Isaacs said, labeling the old system deplorable, "that the publishers were former circulation managers or advertising managers, and the people who ran the print shops and the advertising managers got far more money than the editors did. That has changed dramatically over the years."

Impact

The estrangement between practitioners and academic researchers has often made communications research irrelevant, according to the academics. "I don't think it does any good for a number of us to devote countless hours and a lot of money and time to communication research if it doesn't have the chance of having much of an impact on the way communication works in society," Gerbner said. What communications researchers wanted, Bogart explained, was "to get ideas and information talked about, thought about, and then thrust into practical application." This rarely happened, Levy commented.

Even the small amount of research that did come to the attention of editors and publishers, Weaver said, didn't ordinarily trickle down in news rooms. Isaacs and Ismach agreed. "There's almost a total absence of any intercommunication within news operations," Isaacs said. "Nobody ever even tells anybody anything of what they read."

In general, the academics blamed the lack of any working relationship between researchers and professional communicators on industry, saying that media practitioners did not want to risk hearing criticisms of their operations so were only receptive to studies whose outcomes could lead to prospective increases in revenues. In rebuttal the practitioners said that making money was a necessary activity in the business world. Furthermore, they insisted, it would be folly to let research control editorial decisions for newspapers and the electronic media. Still, they reminded, academic studies might have greater currency if only they were written in plain English.

"I have a great love and respect for journalism," Ismach said, "and I wish there were a greater appreciation by journalists of their supracommercial role in this society so that some other nonpragmatic, nonmarketing oriented concerns would exhibit themselves more often. But there seems to be less of that, less tolerance for it than I would expect."

Wackman pointed to the Surgeon General's concern about violence in society and the resulting investigation that brought together representatives of the public, government, and industry. He did not see, he said, any indication of strong industry interest in pursuing the crucial questions that were raised. "To most of us it appears as rather clear-cut evidence that the work on violence has simply been set aside by broadcast management because it conflicts with what is considered to be good program values and audience attraction. So, there is not merely a difference of outlook involved here but really serious conflicts of interest that we have to face up to."

Bogart recalled a similar situation in the past:

Let me go back to an earlier era in which academic research twenty-five years ago was content analyzing the mass media, calling attention to the treatment of minority groups or their absence altogether from the mass media. This was the subject of innumerable papers at scholarly meetings, but nothing happened in terms of the broadcast policy of limiting minority characters on the air and certainly not presenting them as performers, let alone as newscasters. What changed, of course, was the political climate. It was pressure that caused a change in policy. So here we're not talking simply about a difference of perspective between the academic researcher and the media manager; we are talking about an absolute conflict of wills.

As in the case of minorities and the mass media, oftentimes there were practical lessons to be derived from subjects that practitioners might perceive as having no relevance to their day-to-day operations, the researchers pointed out. Bogart reminded conference participants of another issue—media credibility—that he said researchers were interested in long before those in the media were. Academic researchers, he said, were studying credibility for twenty years before editors and publishers found the alienation of audiences from the mass media to be an issue of practical concern. "There are other such issues lying below the surface now that practitioners simply aren't responsive to," Bogart added.

Boccardi objected to the view that industry was overly focused on making money:

> Sure, the communications business is a business. I come out of a failed newspaper so I can give you all the testimony you want about how the noblest motive can become empty pretty quickly. But if you go to state Associated Press meetings or meetings of the ASNE [American Society of Newspaper Editors] or APME [Associated Press Managing Editors], you hear a great deal of conversation about the societal issues and what role we're playing and what social responsibility we have. I am uncomfortable at these repeated references to ours as a business that is only concerned about making money.

Furthermore, Stanton said, making money was not necessarily the antithesis of social responsibility:

> The marketplace is the best regulatory mechanism that we have. It's far superior to all the other mechanisms. And in the long run a rational business run for profit, if the market is working, ought to serve the community and ought to serve citizenship. If you want to put the credibility business in the framework of a dollars-and-cents issue, then, sure, it's a problem if people don't believe you and turn away from your newspaper. Before you know it, you don't have much of a newspaper.

When the executives of the communications industry had gotten interested in the credibility issue, a number of participants pointed out, that interest had led to two studies—one by the APME and the other by the ASNE[4]—both of which had received widespread industry attention and had led to changes in industry practices. Weaver saw the studies as models for future investigations.

The reason the two studies had been effective, several participants said, was that they were joint efforts by industry and academia. This was the best way to get things done, they said. "Why have the ASNE and APME studies on credibility had so much impact or currency?" Boccardi asked. "It may be that since some of us had a role in these studies they were more attended to. Maybe there was something in the kind of questions that were asked, and editors had something to do with that."

The general response was that involvement bred interest. "If a client asks research for an answer," Stanton said, "the chances are that the client will pay more attention to it than to an answer that comes freely given from some other source including an academic setting." Wilkins echoed that opinion. "If you get people involved in the process, they become involved in the results," she said. "It's as simple as that."

However, Keith P. Sanders, professor of journalism at the University of Missouri and associate editor of the *Mass Comm Review*, cautioned conference participants against jumping to conclusions prematurely. "I think it might be presumptuous to assume that there has been a greater impact from the ASNE and APME studies than from previous credibility studies," he said. "We have been studying this at the University of Missouri, and I think it is too early to make that assessment. I don't believe either one of the recent studies really dealt with credibility."[5]

Boccardi reacted to Sanders' statement by saying that regardless of the impact in the long run, the two recent studies did have a currency that other research had not achieved. "The industry is aware of the findings of these studies and people are talking about them to a degree that I think has not been true of other work."

Funding

The lack of industry interest in academic research not only could be felt in terms of impact, researchers said, but also could be counted in dollars and cents. Most saw industry as unwilling to invest in academic research, which they considered both unfortunate from a societal view and short-sighted from a more selfish vantage point. Furthermore, even for market-oriented research, the professors noted, industry was turning away from academic researchers in favor of hiring commercial ones, especially those with business or management backgrounds.

Dennis and several of the practitioners, however, spoke up to defend the industry's support of education and certain research projects, and Donald Brenner, associate dean of the University of Missouri School of Journalism, cautioned against a "coin box campus" mentality. "We should not assume," he argued, "that research questions and answers are useful and important just because somebody is willing to pay for them."

Nonetheless, most of the academic researchers at the gathering chastised industry leaders for not financially backing academic research, complaining that this left academics with the burden of investigating issues of crucial importance to society without adequate funding. "I do think communication researchers are in a bind these days," Weaver said. "We find funding support from the government being drastically curtailed. There are few foundations to support our work, especially programs of research over long periods of time." Weaver, however, was not convinced that the situation was irreversible. "I just hope that in the future those of you in the communication industry will find our work valuable enough that you will step in and help to fill that gap and provide us some support for the kind of research that we need to keep doing in academia." If industry provided funds, he said, that might have an added benefit. It might stimulate an industry interest in the research projects themselves.

Margaret T. Gordon, director of the Center for Urban Affairs and Policy Research at Northwestern University, agreed with Weaver that resources were shrinking and suggested that researchers cooperate rather than compete with each other to make the most of what funds were available:

> I'm telling you, there is not a lot of money out there. And with what I am reading about budget cuts and balanced budgets and so forth, it isn't likely that there is going to be a whole lot more. We have to come up with cooperative mechanisms that allow us to work together on these projects with the available money and not expect that there is going to be a whole lot more available.

Gerbner underscored Weaver's concern about the scarcity of financial backing for long-range projects:

> The most important impediment to cumulative research is the sporadic nature of funding. It's very seldom that researchers, or a group of researchers, have the opportunity to follow through over a period of five to ten years, which is a kind of minimal period for cumulative findings. So what has to be done now is essentially to patch together one-shot projects by different people at different times under different circumstances, which creates methodological obstacles and impedes the cumulative nature of the work.

Several of the academicians were skeptical that the communications industry ever would fund basic research into the larger social questions involving communications and wanted to know why the practitioners had so little interest them. "Why," Ismach asked, "will the media industry not generally support basic research as other industries do—in aerospace, in medicine, in what have you? Does it have to be only the government and the academic community that pay for that very essential spade work?"

Cony conceded that if academicians were looking to industry to support basic research "it would probably be a tough sell." "I don't think my organization would go in on that in any major way," he said.

Boccardi doubted that industry would ever become the major supporter of academic research, but at the same time he reminded conference-goers that the industry had footed the bill for the APME and ASNE studies. He also reminded the academics about funding organizations affiliated with the industry:

> There is foundation money. There are a growing number of foundations fathered by communications organizations. The Gannett Center is an outstanding example. The Advertising Bureau does an enormous amount of work in the research area. So, it seems to me that the industry to some degree is financing some of this research.

Bogart added that researchers could also seek funds from organizations and institutions outside of the communications field.

Although concurring with Weaver that not enough money was being spent on communications research, Dennis saluted certain industry contributions:

> It's unfair to say that the major contribution of the industry has been 100-K or 200-K here or there. The building we sit in and the program here at Syracuse has something to do with the Newhouse organization. There is the Annenberg Program. My program has an initial grant of $15 million to work with. Furthermore, creative people are getting money. David Rubin, for instance, has got money from the Carnegie Foundation to do his project on studies of war and peace in the news media, and there are dozens of other examples around the country. It's not a totally discouraging picture. There is a lot money, and what there is can be used more creatively.

George Comstock, S. I. Newhouse Professor at Syracuse University, backed up Dennis:

> One of the marvelous developments of the last couple of decades has been the investment of the mass media in education as exemplified by the Annenberg School, the Gannett Center, the Newhouse School. In that sense industry has done its part. However, it has perhaps not done its part in terms of research as an endeavor as opposed to education and institutional bases for scholarly activity.

Ismach was not satisfied with the explanations. "Leo, maybe you can speak for the industry," he said to Bogart:

> Is there not a responsibility with the smallest news organization and the largest news organization to support that larger effort that is not self-serving in the immediate sense but somehow contributes to the search for knowledge, to Fred Yu's questions that are transcending and have nothing to do with nuts and bolts? Why doesn't this very profitable thirty billion dollars-a-year industry put together one hundredth of one percent of its revenues or net to go toward these studies?

"Why single out the mass media business?" Bogart asked in response. "Why not suggest that the chemical business or the tobacco business put aside X percent of their funds to solve some of the problems that they collectively create? We all know the answer to that question. You can define what answers professionals want by what they are willing to pay for."

Academicians were wrong, Bogart continued, if they believed that the solution to the funding problem lay in convincing the people who ran the media they ought to be making more of an investment in basic research and using university research facilities as a vehicle for it:

> It seems to me that it is precisely the areas that the media won't in their own self-interest touch that are the proper domain of university research, the domain that encompasses the larger issues of social policies and mass communication that no media organization is going to want to look at. Who is going to sponsor studies that may be critical of the mass media? Who is going to be able to look at a situation and let the chips fall where they may? It's got to be somebody without an axe to grind, somebody from the world of academic or independent research.

Funds for research into societal issues have to come from elsewhere, Bogart said. "That is why we have a government. That is why we have social institutions that will do for us collectively what none of us individually is willing to do. We're talking about a diversity of funding sources." Bogart did concede, however, that securing funds to investigate the larger social policy issues was a problem.

Gerbner maintained, however, that external constituencies provided a "rich picture of research opportunities":

Sources of funding are not limited to the communications industry. In fact, the industry is probably one of the smallest of them in comparison to the National Science Foundation, to the National Institutes of Health, National Institute of Mental Health, to the various professional organizations, to many of the other foundations and mission-oriented organizations. Each project can serve the purposes of the research as it meets the interests of the funder, and this is a tapestry that provides many opportunities into which people can fit very neatly.

Gordon was less pleased with funding opportunities, bringing up a case in point to show the kind of obstacles that often plagued academic researchers:

We have a Northwestern University project on investigative journalism and its impact on public policy, and I am telling you that this project is threatening to media and government and foundations. We have had a terrible time getting it funded although we certainly have had no trouble getting the output of it published in respectable scholarly journals. We did get money from our university research board because they thought it was good. But when we went to foundations, each had a separate excuse.

Isaacs asked if she were suggesting that potential funders had been intimidated by the prospect of media criticism. "Yes, absolutely," Gordon replied. "They were afraid of being attacked by the press."

The communications industry did commission some creative research, if not basic research, several of the conference-goers pointed out in the industry's defense. Isaacs and Wilkins recalled a study that the Roper Organization had done in Kentucky when Isaacs was editor of the Louisville *Courier-Journal*. "The time setting for this was the 1960s," Wilkins began:

At that point racial problems were enormous in a number of cities. They had not been that great in Louisville, and Norman wanted to find out what the climate of that city was. Our study asked people throughout the community how they felt about certain things, how they behaved, where they lived, what they did. It was not a racial study, but the answers that came back showed us that people lived in two different towns in that city.

Now, that study was totally sponsored by the newspaper. And it had very little to do with the newspaper or with communication *per se*, but it was undertaken by the paper and was published by the paper for the city. I do consider it one of the most fascinating studies I have ever worked on. It was sociological research sponsored by the media, which apparently had some applications.

Although the Louisville project could not really be classified as basic research, Bogart said, it did represent "a newspaper editor's imaginative realization that what reporters cover in terms of day-to-day reportage can be seen against a wider backdrop." It also showed, he went on, that there was no need for those in news management to be surprised by political developments that specialists in the field could see coming.

Inside Academia

The preponderance of discussion at the conference concerned outside forces that hampered academic research. However, the conference participants did also consider conditions within academia that they saw as injurious to the research effort. Some blamed the university structure, while others faulted the researchers themselves for their limited vision.

Perhaps the biggest complaint was that the researchers not only had to contend with inadequate funding and with media professionals who paid them no heed, they also had to fight universities that did not value communications as a subject of study. This brought up Dennis' statement quoted in Isaacs' book, *Untended Gates: The Mismanaged Press.* "Mass communications is central to the functioning of society," the passage goes, "but I can't think of a university that acts as if it was."[6] As a result of this, Dennis added at the conference, communications scholars had little clout within universities and their efforts often were depreciated. He did think the state of affairs was improving, however.

Isaacs found this situation within academia deplorable. "Communications has become an unwelcome intruder for many in academic life," he said. "They look down on it as a nondiscipline, and I consider that attitude as noxious a form of protecting turf as any under the academic umbrella."

Because communications had not hewed out a central role in the American university system, it had not shared fully in the resources, according to both Isaacs and Dennis. Communications as a subject of study simply did not have the manpower to grapple with great societal issues. The number of communications faculty members nationwide was not great, and many of these were burdened with other assignments, they said.

Nonetheless Dennis scolded the communications professors:

I would submit that 400 to 600 faculty members in this country in communication schools are in default of their contracts for not carrying out research for which they are paid. I realize there are heavy teaching loads, but every faculty member on a tenure track in every university in the country has a responsibility to do research, and most of them are not doing it.

Meyer brought up another problem with the university structure—a reward system, which, like in industry, discouraged researchers from tackling long-range problems. "In academia," he explained, "someone seeking tenure wants to publish as quickly as possible. So the temptation is to get just enough data to barely qualify for publication and to rush into print with it."

The continuity of academic research was another subject brought up by conference participants. While a number of them admonished researchers for not working together and for not building on each other's research, other participants said research was by nature a solitary activity requiring independence. Several of the participants, including Dennis and Wilkins, saw research as collaborative, solitary, *and* artistic, all three. Wilkins described it as "art using scientific techniques."

Meyer found the demands of researchers to be somewhat contradictory. He agreed with Weaver's argument that communications research had not been cumulative enough:

Many things are done in isolation so that one thing doesn't build on another. Thus the question becomes what is the best institutional way to cure that. Centralizing the funding so that the people who control the funds can encourage researchers to make their work relate to that of others might be one solution. But, of course, there is a trade off. If you go too far in that direction, then you lose the pluralism of lots of different minds doing lots of different things, and I am not quite sure how to strike the balance.

Stanton reacted to Meyer's statement. "If my experience counts for anything," he said, "I would take my chances on the pluralistic rather than the centralized approach. It would have a stultifying effect on research if you were to restrict it that way by the funding routes."

After discussing the problem of freedom versus order, most conference participants seemed to agree that freedom was an essential condition for high-quality research to take place, but at the same time researchers had to be encouraged to build on the work of each other.

McGrath said that she did not want to speak against diversity or pluralism but did "like the idea of having a forum to at least set an agenda." She explained, "different people could then get together but still approach topics in different ways, from the pragmatic to the very theoretical."

Sanders also supported the idea of a forum although at the same time stressing the necessity of pluralism. He began by arguing that research was an activity rather than a product:

> It's what researchers do. We've been talking here in terms of solving particular kinds of problems and generating particular kinds of information, totally overlooking the idea that research is something that we do to answer some questions and frankly to have a lot of fun.
>
> There are a lot of reasons that we might get involved in this activity—to get tenure or pay—but as soon as one begins to outline and assign topics and say you are going to take on the job of doing this, that is producing a product. Then it really impinges upon the activity. It essentially eliminates the creativity involved. The history of science will show that there have been more serendipitous findings of value than any other kinds. You don't plan science.

What needed to be done, Sanders went on, was to get researchers thinking about broad issues in the same way that they had recently been thinking about ethics. A number of academic and professional meetings on ethics, he said, had served to focus thought on, and stimulate interest in, the subject. As a result, he said, several scholars had written books on the subject:

> So ethics is an interesting model. There really was no body of literature and particularly no philosophy underlying what we were doing. Now, I think we're moving into an era where we'll be able to deal with ethical problems for at least the next fifty years on a much sounder basis. A lot of interesting things have gone on or are now going on because there was a facilitative mechanism to bring scholars and other people together to engage in a creative process but not to direct anyone to produce a paper on this or that by the end of the year.

Gordon said more cooperation was going to be necessary in light of the paucity of future funding. "The foundations are concerned about turf battles," she said, "and are desperate to find ways to get people to work together." She conceded that this might be a difficult goal to attain.

The desire for uniqueness among academicians might also make cooperation difficult, according to Judith D. Hines, vice president of the ANPA Foundation. There were few rewards in academia for collaborators, Gordon reminded.

Although stressing the need for research to be cumulative, with investigators challenging or extending the work of their predecessors, Gerbner nonetheless opposed the formation of any institution or mechanism to try to order researchers or research topics. He feared that any attempt to streamline communications research would oversimplify the subject and straitjacket researchers:

> I don't think such a mechanism would be desirable. If anything, we need more diversity and a greater number of agenda settings at the same time, not fewer. I can understand how anybody with a fairly single-minded interest would like to see things more coherently organized, but this would impose a constraint that would on the whole result in a reduction of research, not an increase in the richness of options and alternatives available.

Yu also was concerned with encouraging pluralism, but more in terms of methodology. Continuing the discussion he began in his paper, he suggested that too much attention was being focused on methods, *per se,* and that some of these—survey research in particular—were being overused:

> I, myself, have been too comfortable just being content with using a few of the tools we have borrowed from the shelves of a few disciplines. There are a lot of other shelves that we should look at. I do not quite agree that methods are important in and of themselves. I much prefer to talk about problems. Once you agree on the problems you want to study, you then try somehow to find methods. I think we started with survey research because of one of our founding fathers, Paul Lazarsfeld. It was an important method. It still is. But I think media research people have sort of gotten hung up on survey research. It is not the only—or even the main—research method. There are other approaches. There is no end or limit to the number of approaches that could be taken to the study of mass communication.

Methodology also was a concern of Gordon, who said she found the research reported in *Journalism Quarterly* to be less sophisticated than she would like. "People are talking about *Journalism Quarterly* being impenetrable," she began. "But sometimes, even if you can penetrate it, you won't feel like you've learned a lot. I think there's a need to do projects that involve multiple methods, but that is expensive."

Proprietary Research

Although commercial researchers worked on studies that professionals were willing to pay for and, thus, presumably cared about, these researchers said they often faced problems similar to those described by the academics. Hines implied that even proprietary research sometimes received little attention or had little impact when she questioned whether newspaper executives or professors had ever heard of the comprehensive Newspaper Readership Project conducted and supervised by Bogart.[7] "I am aware that the Newspaper Readership Project has a great library of research, and I think what Leo did amounted to a milestone for research in our business and some agenda settings," she said. "But my sense has been that there were a lot of people in academia who were not aware of it although Leo really tried hard to make it public. It seems to have disappeared from the face of the earth."

Dennis assured her that the research had had an impact as it was now quoted in college textbooks for communications courses. "So, virtually every reporting course in the country acknowledges the existence of those studies, what they meant," Dennis said.

"I'm delighted that students are learning about these studies," Bogart quipped, "because editors haven't." Bogart went on to expain how his research had been ignored or disregarded. Studies he worked on in the early 1970s looking at why people read newspapers, he related, showed they did so to get news as opposed to entertainment and that they were becoming more interested in national and international news than local news:

> Anyway, during the period since we first reported these results to editors, newspapers have continuously moved in the direction of increasing the ratio of entertainment to news—hard news—and increasingly in the direction of local as opposed to national and international news.
>
> I understand there are excellent reasons that can be given for these trends —specifically (1) the total news hole has increased so that the absolute amount of space devoted to both hard news and to national and international news has not declined, and (2) there has been a desire on the part of editors to improve their products by having more stories staff-written and not picking up a large amount of boilerplate and wire service material. But, whatever the reasons, the fact is that we have seen newspapers move progressively further away from the conclusions shown by the empirical research.

Another problem, however, bothered Wilkins more and seemed to her to be more intractable. It was the secrecy that shrouded proprietary research. "We ought to be talking more," she said. "Sometimes I am struck by how many of us are doing the same thing. That bothers me a great deal. Sometimes we think we have come up with a wonderful idea for a research project, and we go and do it, only to find out that several other people are making similar studies." Gordon agreed: "Even at meetings of the Newspaper Research Council, which is made up only of researchers working on newspapers, there still is not necessarily an open sharing since many of these people are competing with one another and will only talk about work that already somehow has become public."

McGrath said that the proprietary research that she had had the opportunity to see was far less superficial than a lot of the people at the conference were suggesting. "There is a lot of basic research about the communications process going on," she said. "There is a lot of theory that is being developed, but it is hidden. It's proprietary." Wilkins added that those who did proprietary research didn't just take somebody's questions, put them out, and publish the results with their names on it. They wouldn't have a name if that was all they did, she explained. Instead, contract researchers helped to shape the research projects that they undertook.

Meyer said he wished there were a way to change the reward system so that people in the industry had an incentive to publish information as now the reward system worked the opposite way. "If you keep information secret, that makes it seem important," he said. "The academic slogan 'publish or perish' would be a good one for private industry."

Bogart, however, claimed that much information eventually did in fact pass hands via networking. "While there is a lot of interesting information that does not get public, there is not very much wisdom that does not get public," he said.

Recommendations

The final morning of the conference, participants worked hard to come up with specific recommendations to alleviate the problems they had been grappling with and to create an atmosphere conducive to high-quality research — one that would, as it was put by Comstock, engender more congenial and productive relationships between the academy and industry. It was often suggested that since the S. I. Newhouse School of Public Communications at Syracuse University had taken the initiative in focusing attention on the subject by organizing the conference, it would be fitting for the school to continue to take the leading role in the effort to find solutions to the problems.

Looking at the gap between the academy and industry, the majority of the conference-goers recommended more conferences, fleshing out proposals that they had advanced more tentatively the day before. Others called for more research projects in the pattern established by the ASNE and APME studies — ones that would take advantage of the resources and talents on both sides of the "grand canyon." Various publications, a data bank, and faculty internships were among the numerous other suggestions offered.

Wilkins proposed surveying academics and professionals to solicit their ideas for improving research and the research climate in the communications field. She and McGrath also recommended a strategy for getting executives to read research findings. The answer, they said, was for researchers to report their results in two versions, one a readable summary for the journalistic community and the other a technical account for fellow researchers.

Rubin said a computer data base on communications research probably could be developed. If it included proprietary entries in addition to academic ones, it might facilitate networking, he said. "It would seem to me," he said, "that we could encourage the media people [proprietary researchers] to at least list their research topics so that there would be a point of entry on getting information. You could at least call about it. I think you could open a lot of doors that way, and it wouldn't be terribly expensive."

A member of the conference audience, Vernone Sparkes from the faculty of the Department of Television, Radio, and Film at Syracuse University, advocated bringing professors into the workplace. Sparkes proposed the creation of year-long research internships within the industry for faculty. Universities would be reluctant to pay for them, he said, so industry would have to create these opportunities.

Stanton said he had had experience at CBS with internships of this sort:

> We've matched the income the researcher would have gotten, and given the researcher access to the company for two or three semesters. An arrangement like this does not have to cost a university anything. In fact, CBS had a history professor from Columbia come down and sit with the people on program practices. In that case, it did not even have to do with research. But it was of interest to him, and CBS wanted to get the experience he could bring to the other side of Madison Avenue.

The participants also looked at collegiate coursework in communications, with Stanton and Bogart recommending that professors train their students to read and analyze communications research articles so that they would be able to inform themselves about research in the field during their careers.

Dennis had another idea for academicians. He asked conference participants to consider the kinds of academic arrangements that made for the best communications research. Since intellectual leadership was an important ingredient in encouraging more involvement in research by faculty, he suggested research councils be set up within communications schools. These councils, he said, could meet several times a year to "diagnose the intellectual interests of faculty and help them channel those interests along the lines that would be most productive for them, whether that was a theoretical direction or a more applied direction." Dennis said that conferences could also be held. Schools could convene their faculties once a year to talk about research, he said.

Joint Research Projects

Just as he did in his paper, Weaver enthusiastically endorsed research projects involving both academics and professionals, citing the APME and ASNE credibility studies as models for what he hoped would be a series of future cooperative efforts. Joint studies, he said, involving both academics and professionals at the planning stage and making results accessible immediately upon completion of the work, represented a way for industry and academia to work together to collect and analyze data to answer questions that would otherwise be too expensive for academic researchers to tackle by themselves. Data tapes from the APME and ASNE studies, he said, continued to be a rich resource for academic researchers.

In line with this Weaver voiced the hope that some media organizations like the ASNE and APME would get together and fill the gap that had been left by the termination of the ANPA News Research Center. "That was a valuable program," he explained. "It produced six or seven different grants a year to academic researchers. They weren't particularly large grants, but they were important sources of funding for work with both theoretical and practical implications, and we don't have that now." This could include, he went on, the establishment of a research center that not only awarded small grants to researchers but also sponsored sessions—going along with the conference idea—at which researchers could discuss their findings and the implications of those findings with people from the media.

Comstock suggested an unusual way of initiating a joint research program that, he said, would "turn the world on its head" and reduce the anxiety industry executives shared about academic research:

> Usually a school comes to the industry in a beseeching manner for funding. It would be interesting, I think, to turn that around and have the school or a set of schools, two or three, come to the industry with money. Now, the goal of this would be to involve industry people, executives and researchers, with academics in joint projects that would go through the normal scholarly and academic channels—that is be open, published, and available.

As Comstock envisioned such a program, the studies would be supported by matching funds from academia and industry and would be carried out cooperatively by academic and industry researchers.

Publications

Several different kinds of publications, including ones summarizing the proposed conferences, were suggested. Boccardi said he would find a quarterly newsletter describing and interpreting the articles in scholarly research journals useful. He suggested that Syracuse University sponsor it. "It could gather the best research that has been done," he said, summarize it, and try to relate it to the professional world. You might have to give that newsletter away for a year or two. But there would probably come a point, if it were good, where you could sell subscriptions to defray expenses, break even, or maybe even go beyond that."

Reinsch gave a telecommunications slant to Boccardi's idea. "As a project for the students in television production, you might consider doing a video cassette of the idea that Lou has proposed," he said. "This would give them a worthwhile professional project to work on. I would suggest that you consider the video cassette in addition to the printed material."

Bogart and Dennis saw the need for another kind of publication. The communications field, the latter pointed out, was lacking a journal with the stature of the *Harvard Business Review*, in which a great deal of proprietary research was in some way refined and much of its yield reported in fairly short order, at least to the business community. "It would be an enduring heritage of this conference," Bogart said, agreeing with Dennis, "if we could establish a journal of proprietary research."

Conferences

The idea endorsed by the largest number of participants, however, was to hold more conferences. It was McGrath who first brought up the subject of these future gatherings whose objective would be to at least set agendas. Representatives of various organizations and academics could get together, she said, to look at questions of interest, share information, and discuss ways — from the pragmatic to the theoretical — of researching questions. "Topics," she said, "could range from the very practical—what are we going to do about young readers; the entertainment section in newspaper X—to very large societal issues like the knowledge gap. And interested researchers could approach the same agenda items in different ways and with multiple points of view."

The key, according to Bogart, would be to establish conferences on specific rather than general topics:

> In the media world, which is already over-saturated with meetings and forums and seminars and conventions and conferences, there is a resistance to having yet another seminar on any particular subject. But if we want to make progress in applying what we know about, say, young people's readership of newspapers or old people's watching of late night television shows, then there's no better way of doing it than through the mechanism that we are using here.

Following up on the conference idea, Stanton proposed that Syracuse University commit itself to sponsoring yearly conferences, bringing together academics and professionals, for the next ten years. "That would go a long way toward establishing a bridge between the academic world and those of us who come out of the so-called 'real' world," he said. "I'm not suggesting that the same participants be involved each year, but I think with skillful selection and with some overlap from year to year a body of relationships could be developed that might be very useful."

McGrath continued exploring the conference idea, recommending a two-day annual conference format, with the first day devoted to examining one particular narrow subject from many different viewpoints and the second day earmarked for a more general discussion:

> Realizing that there are going to be many different drummers in different areas of research working on individual projects, I am sort of working off the idea of a yearly conference devoted to studying topics of inquiry that people perhaps would know about a year in advance. This would provide a topical focus that people could explore from multiple points of view— everything from the symbolic environment that Dean Gerbner has been talking about to the very nuts and bolts things that a lot of other research is involved with.
>
> The finding, for example, that there is an incredible ignorance of public affairs issues among young people, particularly women from the ages of eighteen to twenty-five, might be one topic. Others could be media fragmentation versus media consolidation or the knowledge gap (the idea that perhaps there no longer is equality of opportunity in terms of access to information with all the databases that are accessible only to certain people).

Bogart continued to develop the idea of targeted conferences, recommending that each of the sessions be followed by a publication that would make a wider audience aware of the intellectual interchange:

> I would start on a rather small scale. Since *Journalism Quarterly* has been criticized here, why not convene at the Newhouse School a small meeting of the editors of the *Journalism Quarterly* and a handful of representatives of the various media just to spend a day talking about some of the things that we've talked about, the criteria for article selection, and the procedures used for soliciting articles.
> We have talked about the Newspaper Research Council and how outsiders are excluded from its meetings except to give specific papers. That organization, which is formed by about two hundred professional researchers on newspaper staffs, meets twice a year. Why not invite that organization to meet here at one of its annual meetings and on that occasion open the program up wide to anyone who wants to attend.

Such a conference might lead to more interchange between academics and members of the council, Bogart said. It might even lead to an expansion of the organization's membership roles, he added.

Bogart then applied the idea to the electronic media:

> In the broadcast research field, there's only one organization that I'm aware of—the Radio and Television Research Council in New York City—that consists of broadcast researchers who talk about issues. And the issues that are important to them are almost entirely in the area of the methodology of ratings. Occasionally, there is a speaker who gets into systems of program evaluation or some content analysis, or talks about the threat of new electronic forms. That organization, while it has vastly expanded its membership—probably 250 or so people are in it today, all in New York—receives no academic input. There is no infusion of the kinds of ideas and theories that many of the people here could contribute. Why not sponsor a meeting with the members of that group as well?

Wackman wondered whether people in the industry and academics would be interested in exploring the same topics at conferences. "The key to research is the questions you ask," he asserted. "We really need to understand what kinds of questions each set of parties is interested in and see if there are bridging possibilities or not." The first step, he said, would be for practitioners and academicians to exchange ideas with the intention of developing a set of questions of mutual interest.

Conclusion

At the adjournment of the conference, participants were left with a clearer concept of the delineation of roles for academics and professionals in communications research. First, while most agreed that ways to strengthen relationships between those in the two groups needed exploring, they also shared an understanding that total cooperation would be unhealthy because professionals and academics did have – and should have – different objectives. Probably most of the conference participants came to look at the division between the academics and professionals not only as inevitable but as appropriate, and even beneficial. Nonetheless, the academicians must have left with some sense of disappointment in regard to their hopes for increased industry funding for their activities.

"There is a chasm between academic researchers and the industry only if we assume that their aims are identical," Gerbner said. "But these are complementary missions; they're not supposed to be identical in terms of scope, mission, outlook, perspective, and purpose." Although support from industry was always welcome, Gerbner went on, basic research – which had to do with the way communications practices, systems, and processes conditioned human life – more often had been, and would have to continue to be, supported by society in general through organizations such as universities and foundations:

> We have a long-standing research project called "Cultural Indicators" whose goal is to develop a theory about the dynamics of growing up in a television culture from infancy, to see how this conditions conceptions of reality. That, I think, is a very important task. But when you talk to some people about it, their eyes glaze over because they are hard-pressed to see how it can be used for media purposes. And to that extent we cannot expect representatives of industry to be supportive except as citizens or as members of families.

Gerbner also pointed to research whose findings might be threatening to the industry. "Who is going to ask unpopular questions?" he asked – and then answered his own question.

> I would say that this is the complementary – not conflicting but complementary – task of institutions that are financed for that purpose and have a de-

gree, a measure, of freedom—called academic freedom—to protect investigators against the dangerous fallout of letting the chips fall where they may. The only problem about this kind of research is that there is too little of it.

So, it seems to me there is no enormous chasm. There are the usual exaggerated expectations. If you sort this out, you can see that there is an overlap, including research on which industry depends, and then there is research into issues of greater general societal and human importance. These are tasks and missions with different purposes, and I don't see anything wrong with that. Academic research is essentially an intelligence operation. If somebody wants service, which is a different thing entirely, let him hire people and pay for it. Let us not force all research into a single mode.

Ismach and Weaver spoke in a similar vein. "There is not going to be total identity of functions for researchers and for practitioners," Weaver said. "While there is some overlap, we have separate things to do."

"If we can agree on anything," Ismach said, "it should be that we each have worthy and defensible purposes. We can recognize that we have dual and separate objectives and still be willing to appreciate and support each other."

Notes

1. Sauter, who had served a stint as president of CBS News earlier, was appointed to the post a second time on December 5, 1985. However, on September 11, 1986, Sauter resigned the presidency. His resignation came shortly after Lawrence Tisch was named acting president and chief executive officer of CBS Inc.

2. Rubin was referring to the November 19–21, 1985, meeting in Geneva, Switzerland, between President Ronald Reagan and Mikhail Gorbachev, general secretary of the Central Committee of the Communist Party of the Soviet Union.

3. The Newspaper Research Council, with headquarters in Des Moines, Iowa, is a professional organization whose members are limited to those who work for newspapers. It holds two conferences each year restricted to members but the "Notes" that are written afterward are shared with outsiders. The organization also publishes a newsletter.

4. The two studies on press credibility were conducted by Minnesota Opinion Research Inc., (MORI), Minneapolis, under the direction of Kristin McGrath, president. Findings of the ASNE investigation, "Newspaper Credibility: Building Reader Trust," in which members of the public were surveyed, were reported in April 1985. The APME study, "Journalists and Readers: Bridging the Credibility Gap," was completed in October 1985. In the latter, people working on newspapers were the respondents.

5. Researchers at the University of Missouri have developed a matrix or schematic for studying credibility with the intention of carrying out future studies on the issue.

6. Norman Isaacs, *Untended Gates: The Mismanaged Press* (New York: Columbia University Press, 1986), 169.

7. The Newspaper Readership Project, sponsored by sixteen newspaper associations, involved a wide range of activities. Amongst them were a series of research projects conducted from 1977 to 1983 and costing approximately $1.5 million. The core staff for the project was assembled by the Newspaper Advertising Bureau and directed by NAB leaders Leo Bogart, executive vice president and general manager, and Albert Gollin, associate director of research. More information about the effort and its findings is available from the NAB, 1180 Avenue of the Americas, New York, N.Y. 10036.

PART III

Perspectives on Communications Research

The short op-ed style essays that make up Part III deepen the understanding of communications research gained at the conference. In them scholars from throughout North America view communications research from a variety of perspectives. Some discuss the whats, whys, and hows of the research itself. Others show the relationship of the research to its academic setting and to the professional communications world.

George Comstock introduces Part III by organizing research activity into four domains. Benjamin M. Compaine then looks at the identity problems that beset the communications discipline/field of study, while research methods, tools, and objectives are commented upon by John D. Stevens, Philip Meyer, and Oscar H. Gandy, Jr. John P. Robinson calls for the development of a sophisticated survey vehicle so that researchers can collect the data they need in order to come to grips with the Information Society of the late twentieth century.

In examining the university environment, Steven H. Chaffee argues that support for the communications research enterprise at major research universities is dependent on strong professionally oriented courses of study. Melvin L. De Fleur analyzes the social system in which academic researchers operate, an essay that is followed by Alexis S. Tan's satiric piece on one aspect of this system—the judging of articles for scholarly journals. Margaret T. Gordon and Ed Mullins explain how research is performed and encouraged at their schools, Northwestern University and the University of Alabama, respectively.

Finally, a number of the essay writers try to pinpoint the relationship (or lack of it) that exists between the research and professional worlds. Albert E. Gollin shows how and why newspapers have come to rely on staff researchers and consulting firms rather than academic researchers, but he does suggest two avenues for academic newspaper researchers to explore in the future. The frustrations encountered by academics are the concern of Mark R. Levy, Alex S. Edelstein, and Brian Winston, while Gerald Stone and Guido H. Stempel III instruct academics on how some of the problems can be ameliorated. The former challenges researchers to communicate more effectively, and the latter argues that training in research be introduced in undergraduate college classes so that future journalists will be able to inform themselves about research findings. Also looking at the educational curriculum, Arnold H. Ismach makes a case for integrating instruction on communications theory in professionally oriented communications courses. In addition, his piece seeks explanations for professional suspicions of communications research. However, Sharon Dunwoody reminds researchers that the media are not the only audiences for communications research, reporting that she finds scientists to be receptive to, even eager about, her work. And Peter Desbarats describes a Canadian program that serves as at least one bridge over the professional/academic divide.

The Four Domains
of Communications Research

GEORGE COMSTOCK

Four Domains

Communications research is, of course, a complex entity with no universal set of priorities and no short list of "what we really need to know." Although many might prefer a more Balkanized breakdown, it can be divided comprehensively and comprehensibly into four domains. They are: (1) responses to communicatory stimuli; (2) audience behavior; (3) delivery of information; and (4) the media as social institutions.

The pertinent questions and answers differ in these four domains as do the research practitioners and the fields from which they come, the topics, the major issues, the applicable concepts and theories, and, in each case, the substantial literatures.

As one would expect, these domains also are characterized by favored research methods. In the first the experiment in a laboratory setting is most prominent. In the second it is the sample survey, in the third the content analysis and the sample survey, and in the fourth the case study and historical and sociological scholarship.

Responses to Communicatory Stimuli

Psychologists have been the preeminent practitioners in behavioral and cognitive responses to communicatory stimuli research. For example, persons whose academic affiliation identifies them as psychologists have contributed about half of the several hundred empirical investigations of the influence of television and film portrayals on anti- and prosocial behavior while persons affiliated with departments and schools of communications have been responsible for about one-fourth. Thus, the contribution of communications as a field has been substantial, but, as is so often the case with communications research, other fields and disciplines have made as large or larger contributions. Topics include:

- the kind and intensity of mental processing associated with attending to the various media and the implications of such processing;
- factors that determine the skills and abilities needed for attending to the various media and changes in such skills and abilities over time with variations in media use;
- perceptual and attitudinal shifts in the assessment of reality as a function of media exposure;
- the influence of various kinds of media content on thought and behavior; and
- the role of the media as socializing agents in the lives of children.

Audience Behavior

Sociologists and marketing researchers have been most prominent in investigating audience behavior. Of all the domains, this is the principal one in which the media themselves have invested and in which they have taken a strong interest. The A. C. Nielsen Co. and its activities in audience measurement exemplify media involvement, but there are innumerable other firms with a similar purpose operating nationally and locally. Almost certainly no form of communications research has been more consistently pursued by the media than the study of their present, potential, and future audiences. Academics have not been absent, however, as the many analyses falling under the rubric "uses and gratifications" testify. Topics include:

- media use and the demographics of that use;
- determinants of media use as a function of demographics and individual interests and needs;
- processes of choosing among available media options;
- trends in media consumption as a function of available leisure time, media, and financial resources on the part of consumers;
- the public's evaluation of the media—in regard to entertainment, transmission of information, and the serving of the public interest;
- the marketplace reception for emerging media, such as pay and cable television, satellite transmission, video recorders and in-home playback de-

vices, and in-home electronic delivery of newspapers and other traditionally print-based information; and
- the future configuration of the media as the emerging media enter the
  marketplace in a manner seemingly analogous to the entry of television
  in the late 1940s and 1950s.

Delivery of Information

Sociologists, evaluation researchers, students of the news media, and political scientists all have been active in the area of delivery of information, particularly the purposeful delivery by news and public affairs coverage and public
information campaigns. Communications as a field has been quite prominent.
The study of presidential election campaigns and the media's role in them constitutes one major thread of inquiry. Another is the study of the effectiveness
of campaigns designed to achieve some widely acknowledged social good, such
as the encouragement of voting, the use of seatbelts, the elimination of alco-
hol and drug abuse, or the cessation of cigarette smoking. A third is the everyday performance of the news media as monitored by content analyses. Finally,
there is the examination of the influence of highly publicized events on thought
and behavior—a thread inevitably entwined somewhat with the first domain,
as is the formative and evaluative research on public information campaigns.
Topics include:

- media balance, bias, and accuracy in covering topics of public interest and
  controversy;
- the electoral role of the media generally, including that in local, state, and
  national elections—particularly their role in electing presidents;
- influence on voter behavior of projections, predictions, exit polling, and
  similar pre-poll-closing coverage;
- conditions on which influences of the media on attitudes and behavior in
  regard to public affairs and political life are contingent;
- differences among the media—principally newspapers and television, but
  also magazines and radio—in their contributions to public opinion, voter
  behavior and evaluation of candidates and office holders;
- public attitudes toward the media, particularly in regard to First Amendment rights and governmental control and regulation of the media to ensure responsible behavior;
- evaluation of the media in terms of public service;
- the design and evaluation of campaigns to change public behavior; and
- the influence of discrete events achieving prominent coverage by the media.

Media as Social Institutions

Sociologists have been extremely interested in the media as social institutions. So, too, have many scholars who have taken a critical stance toward the media with an emphasis on social structure and the relationship of the media to the society in which they exist. Communications as a field has been quite prominent. Topics include:

- legal, statutory, and regulatory status of the media and the implications for media behavior;
- ownership, control, and economic organization of the media and the implications for media behavior;
- decision making within media organizations in regard to policies and specific content to be disseminated;
- relations between media and government in regard to media content;
- relations between media and government in regard to the coverage given by the media to government;
- relationship of the media to elites and the implications of that relationship for media behavior;
- behavior by media organizations and within media organizations;
- values, ethics, and goals of media organizations and those who work in them;
- the character and makeup of news and entertainment as *de facto* measures of conformity by media personnel to values, ethics, and goals fostered by media organizations;
- sociological, psychological, and intellectual bases of employment in the media; and
- historical evolution of the mass media with the continuing entry of new technologies ever more capable of reaching larger audiences.

Conference Focus

At the Syracuse conference the focus was almost wholly on the second and third domains of communications research, especially the performance of the media in serving the public (and particularly that of the news media in informing the public) and the use of research by the media both to better serve the public and to fare better as businesses by better satisfying audiences.

In addition, the conference sought reforms, as is typical of ad hoc conferences, which are often called into being as part of a search for solutions to problems and often serve as a means by which a field of professional endeavor reaffirms its vitality. The ad hoc conference is a promissory note to the future regarding priorities and goals on the part of the sponsors and participants. Time will tell in what denomination and currency the note in this instance will be redeemed.

One concern among those at the Syracuse conference, as exemplified by David Weaver's presentation, was the diffuse, noncumulative and often trivial nature of so much that has occurred under the label of communications research.

Another concern in the same vein, exemplified by the presentation of Everette Dennis, was the question of substance: have those who do research been asking the right or important questions, have the various clienteles for communications research asked of it what they should have and have they been given what they ought to have been?

A third, exemplified by Frederick T. C. Yu's look into the future, was the slowness with which paradigms within communications research have changed to encompass issues raised by new communications technologies, the increasing roles of informational resources and communications issues in national development and international relations, and the factors that set communications research apart from disciplines such as economics, psychology, and sociology.

Finally, there were persistent complaints about the indifference on the part of media practitioners to the uses they might make of research (with the occasional exceptions of audience measurement and marketing research) and, to a lesser degree, about the lack of sensitivity and insight on the part of scholars, researchers, and social scientists to the interests and concerns of media practitioners.

Two Examples

Because the search for high quality communications research was the overriding concern at the Syracuse University conference, it is constructive to consider two examples of communications research — one that succeeded in its mission and another that failed to live up to its promise. The first is an exception to the non-cumulative, diffuse, and trivial character of much communications research. The second can be said to be a monumental embarrassment both to the commercial or media-supported and the academic research communities. In both instances, the question to be answered is *why*.

Constructive Research[1]

At present, in a number of United States communities, multimillion-dollar experiments sponsored by the federal government in cooperation with other organizations are underway. The experiments use the mass media to propagandize on behalf of improved personal health habits—that is, practices that have been shown to increase well-being and longevity. These include reductions in cigarette smoking, changes in diet, and the adoption of exercise regimens.

The immediate practical precursor is the three-community experiment conducted by Stanford University in which, over a two-year period, a truly massive mass media campaign to reduce coronary risk by changing individual practices not only had some measurable success, but, at the end of the two years, the mass media by themselves were found to have had as much impact on community health practices as did a program in which expensive clinical education and training for high-risk groups was added to the mass media campaign.

The theoretical precursor to this highly practical project is what is called the "health belief model." This hypothesizes that behavior related to risks, such as health and safety practices, can be altered by enhancing the value placed on reducing the risk, increasing the belief that the risk can be reduced, and increasing knowledge about how the risk can be effectively reduced by means well within the capacity of the average individual. One of the ways by which these latter goals can be pursued is through the mass media because what people think about and what they believe in regard to risks (as well as much else) is open to change by new information. That information can be provided by the mass media via news, entertainment, and advertising.

The health belief model, in turn, derives from a formulation known in psychology as social learning theory. This deals with the factors affecting acquisition, maintenance, and performance of behavior when a preeminent influence is the observation of the behavior of others.

Social learning theory has its immediate roots in the laboratory experiments conducted at Stanford University in the early 1960s by psychologist Albert Bandura. In these experiments, the behavior of nursery school children was altered by their exposure to brief film episodes on a television screen. The broad topic of these experiments was the principles of learning that contrast sharply with those posited by reinforcement theory, which would require that behavior occur and be followed by concrete reinforcement for any learning to occur. Their specific focus, however, was the influence of violent television portrayals on the aggressive behavior of young children. These and later experiments by Bandura and others, which share a similar focus and are derived from the same theoretical framework, constitute a major component of the evidence on both whether and in what ways violent television and film portrayals contribute to aggressive and/or antisocial behavior. In turn, this theory and these television-violence experiments have become the basis for an extensive body of research on whether and in what ways television and film portrayals can affect various positive, constructive, or "prosocial" ways of behaving.

Here is an extraordinary instance of varied but hardly diffuse, nontrivial, cumulative research extending over more than two decades in which laboratory experiments with nursery school children on the effects of television violence can be said to be the foundation for multimillion-dollar multi-community experiments to change individual health practices through massive mass media campaigns. Evaluation research now underway will record their degree of success, if any. The key to this extraordinary instance is the strong role accorded to theory in psychology. Thus, reinforcement theory developed by experiments using birds and animals has been and will continue to be applied successfully to human behavior in such widely varying contexts as industry, programmed learning, and gambling. Social learning theory, developed by experiments using young children by analogue, similarly can be applied to a wide range of adult behavior. The latter recently has been relabelled "social cognitive theory" to emphasize that observation of others achieves its influence by altering the understanding an individual has of a mode of behavior, such as its efficacy, applicability, or appropriateness.

The implication is not only that there is more to the story of television violence research than the quantity of studies attesting to media effects (a fact accurately recorded by Weaver), but also that the reason for the anemic nature of much of communications research is not its topic but its insufficient attention to theory.

Misguided Research[2]

It is also constructive to examine a line of research that has foundered. In the past few years, it has become increasingly obvious that the far slower than anticipated adoption of the so-called "new technologies" was highly predictable. The projections that led many to believe that the United States would be 80 to 90 percent cable-wired and that audiences would enjoy a rich, varied diet of narrowcast video ranging from high culture to the lowest of comedy by 1980 (or '70, '85 or '90) derived from a technology-driven model: that which could be done would be done and done most likely as promptly as it could be done.

A more conservative view derives from an audience-driven model that takes into account spending on the media, interests and needs of audience members, program supplies and costs, habits of media use, and satisfaction with available media. Varied and substantial – if somewhat scattered – data indicate that:

- Spending on the media has decidedly finite limits, so that new media can gain only at the expense of old media unless all media become more cost-effective.
- The media are used variously by their audiences depending on the particular features of the medium in question, and television is primarily used as a source of popular mass entertainment.
- Television programming inventories are far too thin and program production costs far too high for narrowcasting of programming sharply distinct from that found on broadcast television.
- Media habits are not readily changed, and television is largely consumed in blocks of time when other commitments and obligations are absent so that programming requiring to-the-minute attention and transfer of attention, as cultural programming implies, is incompatible with the place assigned television by many viewers.
- Satisfaction with the mass media is quite high, selective dissatisfaction can be resolved by selective attention, and those dissatisfied with the content predominant in the mass media can turn to a myriad of other media.

The slow growth of cable, the financial failure of the major cultural services, the financial struggles of other specialized cable services, the public disinterest in the pay-telecasting of Broadway productions, and the short or null appearance of other innovations alleged to redeem the wasteland of broadcast television should have been expected. Analogous comments can be made about interactive cable, teletext, videotex, and other systems for making the American home part of a two-way electronic information network.

Two circumstances have stood in the way. On the one hand, there has been an inability to perceive that there existed a pertinent body of data collected over the past several decades on the relationships—affective, attitudinal, behavioral, and cognitive, as well as socioeconomic or demographic—between the media and their audiences, a reproach most applicable to the academic research community from which sensitive and perceptive interpretation of findings might have been expected. On the other hand, research was essentially partisan in its assembly of data supportive of one or another of the innovations or services, a reproach decidedly applicable to the commercial research community. Thus, the question of poor use of research by the media is not at all academic, and, in this case, the media have paid dearly for their mistakes.

Notes

1. To trace this productive line of research on social learning theory, see the following sources: Albert Bandura, Dorothea Ross, and Sheila A. Ross, "Imitation of Film-Mediated Ag-

gressive Models," *Journal of Abnormal and Social Psychology* 66, no. 1 (1963): 3–11; Albert Bandura, Dorothea Ross, and Sheila A. Ross, "Vicarious Reinforcement and Imitative Learning," *Journal of Abnormal and Social Psychology* 67, no. 6 (1963): 601–7; Marshall H. Becker, ed., "The Health Belief Model and Personal Health Behavior," *Health Education Monographs* 2, no. 4 (1974); George Comstock, "The Mass Media and Social Change," in Edward Seidman, ed., *Handbook of Social Intervention* (Newbury Park, Calif.: Sage Publications, 1983), 268–88; John W. Farquhar, Nathan Maccoby, Peter Wood, Janet K. Alexander, Henry Breitrose, Byron W. Brown, Jr., William L. Haskell, Alfred L. McAlister, Anthony J. Meyer, Joyce D. Nash, and Michael P. Stern, "Community Education for Cardio-Vascular Health," *Lancet* 1, June 4 (1977): 1192–95; J. Phillip Rushton, *Altruism, Socialization, and Society* (Englewood Cliffs, N.J.: Prentice-Hall, 1980).

2. To trace this embarrassing line of new media audience research, see the following sources: George Comstock, "Today's Audiences, Tomorrow's Media," in Stuart Oskamp, ed., *Applied Social Psychology Annual*, vol. 8 (Newbury Park, Calif.: Sage Publications, 1987); Herbert Goldhamer, *The Social Effects of Communication Technology* (Santa Monica, Calif.: The Rand Corporation, 1970); Everett M. Rogers, *Communication Technology: The New Media in Society* (New York: The Free Press, 1986); Vernone M. Sparkes, "The Half Wired Nation: Cable Television's Fifty-Five Percent Penetration Barrier," paper presented to the Broadcast Education Association, April 1984, Las Vegas, Nev.; Richard A. Winett, *Information and Behavior: Systems of Influence* (Hillsdale, N.J.: Lawrence Erlbaum Associates, 1986).

Communications Research: Coping with a Fuzzy Identity

BENJAMIN M. COMPAINE

Much of the frustration of working in communications research is the lack of specificity, or even agreement, as to what communications is as an academic discipline. Or is it a field of study?

Unlike traditional academic disciplines, communications has a multiple personality, one part practical, one part academic. The same schools that train workaday journalists have a mission of turning out research that helps us understand the process in which the journalists take part. That can't be said for departments of history or languages.

Indeed, even the term "communication" has a wide variety of meanings. A help-wanted advertisement in the newspaper seeking a "communications specialist" may be a job description for an engineer who can connect computers over a telecommunications system.

But we don't have to go that far afield to find differences. The Summer 1986 issue of *Journalism Quarterly* has an article of a historical bent ("An Editor Speaks for the Natives: Robert Knight in 19th Century India") as well as a few pages from a pragmatic empirical study ("Gatekeeping and the Network News Mix"). Communication researchers not only tend to employ the techniques of traditional disciplines, but in fact often tend to be historians, sociologists, economists, lawyers, political theorists, or market researchers who happen to apply their approach to subjects with a communications flavor.

The foregoing is meant to be neither criticism nor praise. It is a description. But this fuzziness of what communications researchers do and how they do it does rub off on how outsiders may perceive the field. Practitioners of professional communications—journalists, publishers, advertising and public relations folks, circulation directors, *et al.*—are understandably skeptical of the communications research field in general when they see some of the scholarly output that comes from our schools of mass communication. If such research came from the history or cultural anthropology department, they would ignore it—or most likely not even know about it. But when it comes from a part of the mass communication department or school, they no doubt wonder what these folks are doing that has any relevance for their "real world." Moreover, rightly or wrongly, it may taint the work of the more pragmatic researchers, as all tend to be painted with the same broad brush of "academic."

The "discipline versus field of study" debate is something of a red herring. It does not need to be won by either side. Frederick Yu is probably correct when he argues that communications research is more properly considered a field of study. But George Gerbner can still make a strong case that distinct schools of communication are the best place to apply the eclectic disciplines needed to tackle such a diverse field. Business administration, after all, is in a similar position of being a field without its own discipline, but the business schools have justified their existence as distinctive jurisdictions in which to apply economics, psychology, and assorted other disciplines. And they have been quite successful in carving out a large niche in the academic world while establishing their *bona fides* with the real world.

One small fix in firming the identity of communications research might be the development of more distinct outlets for communications researchers. This is happening; journals such as *Information and Behavior* and *Critical Studies in Mass Communication* are providing readers with a better sense of what type of research to expect between the covers.

If this brief analysis is accurate, there does not need to be serious handwringing amongst communications researchers. Worries about the state of communications research should not really be allowed to drain much of our energy. The research agenda is determined by the marketplace—both commercial and academic. An emphasis on empirical, pragmatic research today gives way to historical perspectives and social agendas tomorrow and then back again. Graduate schools teach alternative methods of research and analysis. And their graduates will continue to research what they like and what they think is needed.

Are We Saying Precisely Nothing?

John D. Stevens

Three decades ago, Frederick Siebert urged communication law scholars to do "more case studies and fewer studies of cases." He said readers needed to be told about the defendant and why the prosecution was brought, not about which justices agreed on an arcane point in the decision.

Tell us what it means, he implored. It is time to raise that cry again—and to all communication scholars, not just those in law. Too many of us have substituted precision for significance. Like good trial lawyers, we seldom ask a question to which we are not sure of the answer. Our results, all placed in tables and carried to the third decimal point, usually confirm what most people have figured out for themselves. No wonder they pay so little attention to much of our scholarship.

Perhaps because of our inferiority complexes—so often reinforced by colleagues in older, traditional disciplines—we tend to play it safe, electing questions that fit the techniques of "hard" and social science. Many people in our field have learned to use them with sophistication.

Like many other communication scholars whose instincts are humanistic, I had a fling with quantitative techniques. Why not use those skills that we had acquired so painfully in graduate school? Like a kid with a new hammer, I discovered the world was full of things that required hammering. When I discovered myself looking for hammerable topics, I put the old hammer away and since have brought it out only for special tasks. I discovered that planes, screwdrivers, and all sorts of other tools worked better for many undertakings, but I always have tried to choose the tool for the job, rather than the other way around.

The reductionist nature of quantification is appropriate for some kinds of history and useless (or worse) for other types. Quantitative tools are indispensable in economic history, and they have revolutionized social history. Because so few ordinary people leave much in the way of manuscripts or formal records, the social historian is forced to look at large samples of the basic records that nearly everyone leaves—records of births, marriages, and deaths, as well as licenses and taxes. The social historian analyzes masses of such data to reconstruct what was "typical." Some of the findings have been fascinating, giving us insights into how ordinary people lived. They are the closest equivalent for the historian to survey data.

Quantification also is useful in political history, voting results being almost the only indicator of past public opinion. Legislative and judicial votes also can be analyzed endlessly in a computer.

The techniques of quantification have been less successfully applied to intellectual history or biography, especially to the unfortunate sub-species known as psycho-biography. In such fields the scholar must expand and generalize on ideas and individual lives; numbers squeeze out the very individuality and the humanity the scholar wants to emphasize. Humanistic approaches are as valid —and certainly they are much older—than those associated with quantification. Unfortunately for the modern humanist scholar, they are greeted with more suspicion in many journals and by those who referee convention programs.

This is not a numbers-bashing diatribe. Not all humanists ask important questions, but the range they can consider is less limited. Rather it is a reminder to all of us, regardless of scholarly orientation, to keep our priorities straight. "In the beginning was the question."

On the Impracticality of Applied Research

Philip Meyer

In the late summer of 1984, a group of people interested in communications research met in the board room of the Associated Press in New York City to plan a national survey on the newspaper credibility problem. The study was to be paid for by the AP and sponsored by the American Society of Newspaper Editors, and David Lawrence, chairman of the ASNE credibility committee, had wisely included representatives of several constituencies at the meeting. They included newspaper market researchers and professors of journalism.

At one point in the discussion, one of the editors objected to a concession being asked by the academics. "Why do we need these people?" he asked.

"Because," he was told, "we have a longer attention span than you. Credibility was a problem for newspapers ten years ago. It will be a problem ten years hence. We will still be interested in it, still trying to fit pieces of the puzzle together, when you editors have long forgotten it and are pursuing other passing fashions."

The ASNE credibility study was then designed with both past and future research in mind, and it will form part of a cumulative, developing body of knowledge. But most applied newspaper research studies—those designed to reduce the uncertainty in specific, short-term decisions—fail to take into account this cumulative nature of knowledge. Editors overestimate the uniqueness of their problems and underestimate their complexity, and so they settle for single snapshot surveys that pay no heed to earlier work on the subject and form no building blocks for future studies. And there is no shortage of commercial research suppliers eager to get paid for reinventing the same wheel in one market after another.

But the barrenness of applied research in the newspaper business is the fault of neither the commercial suppliers nor their clients. It is due to the lack of a widely understood foundation of basic research on which to build. So little is known about the basic relationship between a reader and his or her newspaper that few editors get past a simple and inappropriate referendum model which says that readers should get whatever the majority of them want.

Even what is known is often unused. For example, researchers have been aware for years that the readership loss of the past two decades has been more one of frequency than of reach. The problem is not to convert nonreaders to readers so much as to get readers to be more consistent. And yet, the over-whelming majority of research commissioned by editors (or at least of the sub-set that I see) continues to treat the reader–nonreader dichotomy as the main dependent variable.

That variable is a poor surrogate for the important ones, which are frequency (for readership studies) or elapsed time as a subscriber (for circulation studies). A snapshot of readers and nonreaders or subscribers and nonsubscribers at any given point in time will show some people who are in each category the moment the snapshot was taken. However, their consistency over time—the important variable—is missed.

For the publisher who wants to build readership and circulation (and who does not?), the task of the researcher is to help him or her allocate scarce resources among the basic variables under a publisher's control: interest in the editorial product, circulation service, and price. Such research could lead to an optimizing equation that would tell the publisher when to shift resources from one of these areas to another so that the marginal benefit from an increment of spending would be equalized among the three. Economists call this the equimarginal principle, and it describes the basic issue of managerial economics. I have never seen it applied in the newspaper business.

Why aren't such studies done? They are risky. No one that I know about has figured out a way to execute one successfully. [For an account of a noble, but failed attempt, see chapter 6 of my *Newspaper Survival Book, An Editor's Guide to Marketing Research* (Bloomington, Indiana: Indiana University Press, 1985).] Such studies require patience, because panel designs, where the same readers or subscribers are followed over time, are required. Newspapers, neither individually nor collectively, have the patience nor the tolerance to take the time and accept the risk.

Some institutional solution is called for. There ought to be an agency that can spend some money on basic research, meaning research for which no application to a short-term decision is anticipated so that subsequent applied research can be made more effective.

What agency? The Newspaper Advertising Bureau comes to mind because of all the newspaper associations it tries the hardest to do the most to produce research of long-term benefit. But it lacks a good institutional or even informal connection to the editor network, and its work tends to be overlooked, perhaps because of the historic antipathy between business and editorial sides, or merely just as a manifestation of the "not-invented-here" syndrome. The American Newspaper Publishers Association is not a good candidate, having abandoned its News Research Center to the exigencies of budget cutting. ASNE may have the will but not the resources.

It may well be time, ironically enough, for the non-profit sector to come to the aid of this declining industry. There are academic researchers interested in the real problems of newspaper publishing, as the response to the ASNE credibility report has demonstrated. Newspaper-oriented foundations are gaining in resources and demonstrating interest in the survival of the institution that created them. A partnership of research universities and newspaper-related foundations could provide the resources, the will to take risks, and the long attention span that the solution of the industry's basic problems requires.

Headlong into the Future toward the Blue Sky of Information Technology with Both Eyes Open

OSCAR H. GANDY, JR.

In 1964, in the forward to his revised English edition of *The Technological Society* (New York: Knopf, 1964), Jacques Ellul appealed to his readers to try to understand the nature of technological phenomena, to understand the ways in which these technologies threatened freedom, and, armed with that understanding, to confront the challenges they represented.

This plea made nearly a quarter century ago is even more relevant today.

The technologies that Ellul identified in the 1960s have not changed substantially. In the 1980s, however, their influence is more clearly visible almost anywhere we choose to look. Those of us who look with some sense of trepidation or alarm are marked as pessimists, or worse, paranoids.

So be it. Too many others are ignoring dangers that need to be faced by society in general and communications researchers in particular.

It is, perhaps, as Marxist political theorist Antonio Gramsci and more contemporary critical theorists have suggested, the nature of hegemony is such that the expanding social constraints associated with the technologies appear as normal, commonplace, and socially justified extensions of longstanding traditional relationships.

How else can we explain the fact that, in an era of widespread testing of bodily fluids and brain waves and of high speed matching of patterns to profiles and of data files to each other, a leading communications scholar like Everett Rogers can all but ignore the massive invasions of personal and group privacy in his latest book, *Communication Technology* (New York: Free Press, 1986)?

Critical theorist Anthony Giddens suggests that, in an age when the computer makes possible an endless variety of means to store, process, and disseminate information, "the possibilities of accumulating information relevant to the practice of government are almost endless."[1] And analysts at the Congressional Office of Technology Assessment (OTA) conclude that changes in information technology have made existing privacy legislation all but obsolete. Yet, they also note that the "broader social, economic and political context of information policy, which includes privacy-related issues, is not being considered" and, given the present nature of the policy process, it is unlikely to be considered any time soon. Apparently nobody has got the time!

Everyone is too busy reeling from the effects of a continuing economic crisis. Changes in the nature of the world economy have served to accelerate the search for productivity gains wherever and however they can be made. Information and information technology have been marketed as the key to unlocking the door to America's economic future. They are seen as providing a relatively reliable and unobtrusive means of monitoring worker productivity. Computers and microprocessors substitute a new kind of capital for labor in the production process. Not only are these new machines tireless, docile, and loyal, but they also possess a high degree of job-specific intelligence already built in.

For those who, as a result of changes in the factory or office, have been temporarily unemployed or are subjected to periodic forced leisure, the same computerized systems are called into operation by the new, more efficient welfare state. "Front-end-verification," involving extensive matching of computerized files, both public and private, is required as a part of each state's assurance of compliance with the Grace Commission's recommendations. The computer has been identified as a front line soldier in the battle to eliminate "waste, fraud and abuse" in the delivery of government social services.[2]

For those fortunate enough to remain gainfully employed and possessed of some disposable income, targeted promotions—fine-tuned in the electronic test markets operated by A. C. Nielsen or by competitors at Behaviorscan or ScanAmerica—are delivered in highly personalized and increasingly effective appeals. The new microwave channels, dual cable systems, and "people meters" linked to universal product code scanners now make it possible for market researchers to produce almost laboratory experimental control within the more natural environment of the American home. When combined with the behavioral minutiae gathered by massive national sample surveys conducted by firms like Simmons Market Research or Media Mark Research, messages can be delivered with a high degree of precision and impact.

At the same time that government and industry learn more and more about the citizen, client, employee, and customer, tendencies toward greater secrecy, privatization, and proprietary exclusions continue to shift the balance of power away from individuals and toward bureaucracies. And, people are not coming together to pool their strengths in efforts to redress this balance. A third of the population is reported not to belong to a single association. Another third belongs to only one. And those associations that have a broad public interest orientation are woefully underfunded and, therefore, underinformed.

The same information technology that is used to market soaps and stereos is increasingly being called into play to more efficiently manage political campaigns and referendum initiatives. The segmentation and targeting techniques are used systematically to exclude individuals, neighborhoods, and groups whose profiles suggest either apathy or wrongheadedness. Thus, the "public sphere," where public opinion is developed through robust debate, is being abandoned in favor of narrow-casting and geodemographic targeting. This no doubt contributes to the continuing decline in electoral participation.

These are, of course, quite serious charges to be hurled in the face of the advancing Information Age. While I am not alone in warning of the collective dangers we face, communications researchers by and large have been swept along by the "gee-whiz" magnetism of high technology. A few of my colleagues do make the obligatory acknowledgement of the growing disparity between the information rich and the information poor. However, very few share the neo-Luddite vision of Frank Webster and Kevin Robins. Their recent examination of *Information Technology* (Norwood, N.J.: Ablex, 1986) makes the necessary historical linkages between much of this technology and the social relations that have brought it into being and constrain its application. Such a perspective helps us to raise questions about what this Information Age really means.

John Vogue, director general of telecommunications for France, has noted that, while there has in fact been an increase in the proportion of the workforce engaged in information work in the United States, the amount of the national product actually consumed in the American household has remained nearly constant. Thus, he points out, the essential demand for information is for the "organization and regulation of the production and distribution" of material goods and services. This suggests that the information economy has so far been limited to efforts to increase productivity within industry and to the area of sales. Limits to further productivity gains may be reached quite soon when the "information" workforce accounts for more than half of the Gross National Product. We need to understand the implications of the Information Age. Even more restrictions on essential rights and freedoms undoubtedly will be imposed in the search for what is left of continually declining marginal returns from investments in information.

Communications researchers must begin now to make serious efforts to understand what this technology really means. They must discover why it was developed, how it is generally used, and how laws and social conventions are being modified to normalize the disruptions it produces.

Notes

1. Anthony Giddens, *The National State and Violence* (Berkeley: University of California Press, 1985), 309.

2. The Grace Commission is the popular name for the "President's Private Sector Survey on Cost Control," which was the subject of lengthy hearings and discussions in and out of government in 1984–85. It was this commission that recommended a great variety of measures "to eliminate fraud, waste and abuse" in the federal budget. See U.S. Congress, Senate Committee on Governmental Affairs, "Oversight of the Grace Commission Report" Hearing, May 9, 1985 (U.S. Government Printing Office, Washington, D.C., 1985).

Nudging Communications Research into the Age of Information

JOHN P. ROBINSON

E conomists, not communications scholars, tell us we live in an information society. We see it reflected in the increased enrollments in communications courses and programs. We also see it in the increased numbers of graduate students and openings for professors of communications. These increases, in turn, have meant increased communications research – research that has become increasingly quantitative in design and analysis.

More interesting and basic questions on the communications/information flow process are being addressed as a consequence. However, the data bases for much current communications research are quite limited, and many of the most interesting data bases on mass communications are inaccessible because they are collected for proprietary, commercial purposes. At the same time, many of these data bases also have problems of discontinuities in time series and representativeness in design.

Thus, in a period of rapid diffusion of new technology, we have no standard verified measures of the rate of public access to videocassette recorders, cable television, or personal computers. Rating services measurements of the public's print or broadcast media usage are subject to changes due to "improvements" in data collection methodology. As an example, the suggested introduction of "people meters" to replace audimeters as measures of the public's TV exposure will mean a fundamental interruption and discontinuity in that time series. We will no longer be able to depend on a standardized instrument to know whether the public seems to be watching more or less television than it did ten or twenty years ago.

However, standardized behavioral measures of technology availability and usage only provide the backdrop for understanding the impact of new communications and information technology in society. We also need to know *how* and *why* these technologies are being used. What new tasks are being done or new type of programs viewed? Conversely, what things are done (programs viewed) less often? Can one get a good sense of how these technologies are affecting the values, attitudes, and cognitions of the American public?

What would be needed to answer these questions is a long-term study dedicated primarily to the questions, concerns, and theories of communications research. The study would build upon—but not be limited by—the positive experiences of longitudinal data series for other academic disciplines. One such data series is the national election studies of the Center for Political Studies (CPS) of the University of Michigan. Another is the General Social Survey (GSS) of the National Opinion Research Center at the University of Chicago. Both have transformed the way in which the disciplines of political science and sociology think about and address fundamental issues in political behavior and public opinion. To this, one might also add the way in which the University of Michigan's Panel Study of Income Dynamics has reshaped micro-economic theories about the dynamics of wealth and poverty.

These data series have become national data resources for these three disciplines, in each case resulting in a common, high-quality data base that eliminates many of the methodological uncertainties that arise when competing theories or hypotheses are addressed using different data bases. While one may wish that the studies produced more "grand theories" of societal functioning, these data bases make it clear how complicated or unrealistic a goal that often is. To the extent that the data fail to address important issues, they are open to improvements and suggestions to that end from the larger scholarly community.

Both the CPS and GSS have included mass communications and information questions in past surveys. But the number and sophistication of these media items are minimal, largely being replicates of items designed ten, twenty, or thirty years ago. No new items are planned, and some existing ones may be dropped. Communications researchers who have worked with the CPS and GSS have spent long, frustrating hours in unsuccessful "lobbying" efforts to add media items that would enhance the ability of both data sets to answer important media research questions and to open new avenues of communications inquiry. We are left with a rather lifeless set of communications variables in these very rich data sets about public opinion.

To be sure, some trend questions about communications technology can be addressed from other sources. The National Product and Income Accounts provide data on expenditures for mass media hardware and software. Time-use studies provide longitudinal data on time spent with print and broadcast media and are being adapted to include time spent with such new technologies as cable TV and home computers. Time spent in interpersonal communications can also be examined. However, these are again only skeletal variables.

What is needed is a survey vehicle more attuned and directed toward our Information Society. Call it, for now, a National Information Survey. Such a survey would first include needed baseline data on the basics of information technology—such as the possession and extent of use of both old and new media and their demographic correlates. But it would also probe into cognitive, attitudinal, and behavioral consequences. What specific information is being processed, not only by owners but by non-owners as well? Are some types of information-seeking increasing, others decreasing? Is there increasing carry-over between use of information technology at the workplace and in the home? Do these technologies increase or decrease feelings of alienation or estrangement between owners and non-owners? Do these technologies enhance or fragment family life? Thus, while the focus would be on "hard" (quantitative) information, it would not be limited to it.

Such a study design could also be expanded to address other issues of long-term interest to communications research, such as the impact of televised violence, advertising, or soap operas. Toward this end, panel features could be incorporated into the study design.

Communications research—and the social sciences generally—largely missed documenting the effects of *the* revolutionary technology of the twentieth century, namely television. At that time, of course, communications research was still in its infancy. That excuse is no longer valid. Many claims about the impact of new communications technology and the Information Society have likely been exaggerated, but not all. This seems an ideal time and opportunity for our discipline to marshall its resources and have a swing at a ball that clearly has landed in our court.

Research As an Academic Necessity

STEVEN H. CHAFFEE

The notion of theoretical research sounds pretentious and irrelevant to the typical mass communication practitioner. Possibly it is. But it is the life-blood of an academic career.

More important in these years of retrenchment in American higher education, faculty research is an essential counterweight to the argument—heard in every university from time to time—that education for journalism and mass communication is a frill. It can, as we are occasionally reminded, be done without. No university would think of abandoning its physics or history department, but a number have consolidated, wound down, or simply cancelled their journalism programs.

A lot of reasons are given for this "pruning," but as a rule the vulnerable journalism programs are those in major research-oriented universities that lack a strong research component. Journalism is, for instance, thriving in the California State University system, which has no doctoral mission, but has been reduced to one or two programs in the more comprehensive University of California system.

Many of the strongest J-Schools are in the midwestern state universities, which offer the Ph.D. in mass communication research alongside professional bachelor's and master's degrees. An ongoing program of research is naturally expected of a professor whose job includes teaching research to doctoral students. This isn't different in principle from requiring significant media experience of those who teach professional skills courses.

But research "productivity"—mostly publication of refereed journal articles—is now expected of many professors in departments that do not offer the doctorate. This is not necessarily an irrational standard from the department's viewpoint. For one thing, many departments offer a master's degree with a thesis requirement; and professors who guide students in current research should also be involved in research. Often a student finds a thesis topic that branches out of a professor's ongoing project.

A larger consideration is that higher administration and faculty in more traditional academic fields expect each department to produce at least some scholarship. This, along with teaching, is a mission common to almost all institutions of higher education. The idea is that students deserve to be taught by people who have themselves contributed to the body of knowledge a college course represents.

Journalism professors and their departments alike have to meet a dual set of expectations. On the one hand, they are supposed to bring professional skills and experience to the classroom, introduce students to writing, reporting, and editing, and keep close relations with active professionals. At the same time, they are measured against the general standards of the academy, which require dreaming up, organizing, and carrying out original research projects. Each department has to maintain an environment where some faculty energy and talent is channeled into each of these competing directions. We can afford to have some professors who specialize in either professional or research pursuits, but it also helps to have "switch hitters" who do some of both. The combination professional–research professor may be the most misunderstood person in the field, never doing enough of either kind of work to bear comparison with those who specialize, and yet essential to holding a dual-mission department together.

Individual professors obviously feel a strain from these competing demands. So do many departments, to the extent that a department can "feel." And so do the larger entities—the profession of journalism and the institutions of higher education—from which the individual and departmental strains derive.

Journalism education cannot avoid the impending crisis. The premium placed on scholarship in the university is growing. More is expected for faculty hiring and tenure at more schools each year. At the same time, the value placed on research by the journalistic profession is at best remaining constant, and low. Regional press associations have attacked what they perceive as research-oriented mass communications programs where they expect more attention to professional skills training. Accreditation is normally a breeze at schools where research expectations are minimal but often a problem at the greatest state universities. What we may soon witness is abandonment of professional journalism education at those major universities where traditionally it has been the strongest.

If that happens, it will not represent a triumph of research over the profession. When the integrated B.A.-through-Ph.D. J-School goes, research in mass communication will go with it, just as surely as will education for the profession. That has already happened at several famous institutions where research in mass communication now pops up only sporadically as a temporary interest of a psychologist, historian, political scientist, or sociologist.

As long as a journalism program is housed in a top university, that institution will expect research of its faculty. This fact often eludes media professionals. But if the professional journalism program is dropped, the higher university administration no longer has an obvious need to staff a mass communication research program. This is only beginning to dawn on career academics.

It may sound apocalyptic, but within a few years the mutual survival of both endeavors—professional education and academic research—is likely to rest upon their capacity to work together, awkward as that sometimes is.

Research Priorities in the Academic World

MELVIN L. DE FLEUR

The papers in the present volume have insightfully probed an impressive number of aspects of the relationship between the research efforts of the academic world and the pressing needs of the media industries for valid findings that will help them meet their goals. Several have noted that a considerable gap exists between theoretically oriented academic researchers and those who need results from more practical research projects. This is an important issue. It is, and probably will remain, controversial. Nevertheless, the continuing examination of the problem is a healthy sign that there may be avenues for the improvement of understanding of the respective needs and roles of academic investigators on the one hand, and the research needs of journalists and broadcasters on the other.

One avenue for improvement of understanding of problems concerning research responsibilities that have arisen between academe and the media industries may be to examine the nature of the norms and social controls within which academic researchers carry out their work. It is my intention, therefore, to set forth in brief a simple description of the social system within which the academic researcher makes his or her decisions to select, pursue, and publish a given research project. That description will reveal no secrets to those in universities; they know the system only too well. It may, however, remind those from the media industries why it may be unrealistic to expect academics to provide readable reports and conclusions that are focused on the pressing issues that they face. The intention is to show that the gap between the two worlds is there because of the operation of a number of inescapable social, psychological, and cultural forces. Unless those are changed in relatively drastic ways, which seems unlikely, the present gap between the two worlds will undoubtedly continue into the forseeable future.

The first principle to recognize in examining the research priorities of academics is that all scientific research, in all disciplines, is conducted within a social, political, and economic environment. That environment influences strongly what scientists investigate, how they get funded, make their observations, write conclusions, and where they publish their reports. The second principle to keep in mind is that academic researchers are human beings. Like all individuals, they have needs for such matters as survival, security, accomplishment, and so on. In addition, most are in family relationships that introduce still other kinds of limitations and controls. For these reasons, such researchers are very likely to comply with the demands of the systems within which they make their livings.

Those social systems and personal factors may seem obvious, but it is the exchanges and rewards prevailing within them that control the decisions made by researchers. For example, the beginner seeking tenure and security by developing an academically significant research project will be unlikely to turn first to the research needs of managers who control the *Boston Globe*, the A. C. Nielsen Co. broadcast ratings, or the Cable News Network (CNN) organization. Instead, the researcher's attention will almost automatically focus on the latest theory or research generalization reported in a technical journal or monograph. The reason is that there are relatively few academic rewards to be obtained in applied research but clear payoffs for pursuing more theoretical problems.

An important factor governing decisions is that most researchers who work in universities hold the doctoral degree. Traditionally that degree has been defined as a research credential. From medieval times to the present it has been associated with the advancement of knowledge—pushing the frontiers forward rather than solving practical problems. Doctoral candidates either accept this as holy writ or seek credentials elsewhere.

For the advanced researcher, as well as the neophyte, the entire social system of academic life is geared to the idea of developing new knowledge rather than to applying principles that are already well known. Virtually every stage in the research process is geared to that interpretation. An elementary examination of the steps involved in putting together, conducting, and publishing the results of a meaningful research project will show how the values of the academic social system shape the decisions that will be made.

First, research topics are frequently selected so as to achieve recognition for the investigator within his or her national community of colleagues. It is by this means that reputation is enhanced, tenure gained, promotions earned, and higher salaries commanded. The universities themselves foster and enforce this tendency by the criteria they exercise in judging people for those rewards. Research on practical issues may be regarded as unimaginative; projects that probe more theoretical issues will be ranked higher.

Second, proposals seeking grant funds for research are scrutinized, not for what the project might do to help media industries, but for what theoretical issues are at stake. Emphasis is also placed on the level of statistical methodology employed. The researcher is expected to use the most sophisticated techniques available. This will scarcely result in an eventual research report that can easily be read by individuals untrained in such methods.

Third, there is intense competition for time slots on the agendas of forums where research findings are presented to peers. Professional conventions screen the papers that are allowed on their limited programs. Those with the most interesting findings from a theoretical point of view have the advantage. Those concerned with more applied problems will have a lesser chance of being included. While the presentation of papers at conventions does not guarantee academic rewards, it does provide one index of the significance of one's research as judged by the relevant scholarly community.

Fourth, research reports submitted to professional journals for possible publication are rigorously refereed. Those who do the reviewing are likely to be theoretically oriented specialists who are intimately familiar with the topics under investigation. Unless the research has been conducted within acceptable limits of methodology, which often means sophistication in statistical analysis, there is every likelihood that the proposed paper will be rejected. In addition, mere description is not enough. Unless some significant theoretical issue is addressed, the paper may have only limited chances of acceptance. Competition for space in the refereed journals is keen, to say the least. The most prestigious journals often reject up to 95 percent of the manuscripts that they receive. Most likely to win approval are those research reports that address frontier issues and use advanced methodology.

Generally, then, the demands of the social system within which the academic researcher makes decisions are likely to channel the individual away from, rather than toward, the concerns of the media manager. These are the facts of life that such researchers understand and live with every day. It should not be surprising that so few research reports are published that have high interest for editors, journalists, and broadcasters. The wonder is that there are any at all! In addition, it should not be surprising that media practitioners have trouble reading and understanding the research reports that make up the majority of those appearing in communication journals. They have, after all, been carefully screened using criteria that virtually ensure that this will be the case.

Is this situation likely to change? Indeed, should it be changed? A good case could be made for a "no" answer to both questions. A number of the essays in the present volume have made an effective case that basic research often provides the applied world with practical ideas and tools. This relationship between basic science and applied interests has been widely discussed and prevails throughout the scientific disciplines.

At the same time, practical media people have good grounds for wondering about the value of much of what is produced by academics. The pursuit of basic knowledge sometimes takes strange paths. No one can deny that. The movement toward a theoretical understanding of some aspect of the communication process can seem like the progress of a drunken sailor, lurching up blind alleys, stumbling over trivia, reeling backwards, and sometimes simply collapsing without ever having gone anywhere.

But genuine progress has been made over the last half century in developing an understanding of both research methodology and principles of communication that have practical value for the business world of the media. It can be granted that the time span between the development of such ideas and their eventual use in applied settings can be a long one. It took many years before the cognitive paradigms of psychology were translated into the "psychographics" of market research. It took an equally long time to realize the value of "demographics" based on the social categories that have long been studied by sociologists. Yet, such gaps are eventually bridged. For this reason, we can only assume that basic research should continue and that the old adage, that there is nothing so practical as a good theory, still has merit.

Why Research Manuscripts Are Rejected

Alexis S. Tan

There are many reasons for academicians to get their work published in the research journals. The most obvious, of course, is continued employment. Other reasons, less obvious perhaps—and less likely to be admitted by many of us—include the following: enhancement of one's "market value," promoting a pet theoretical approach, criticizing a theory we don't like, promoting a social cause, and supporting a favorite peer, former student, or former mentor. And, of course, there is always the motivation to expand knowledge in our field.

Most of us know how it feels to be rejected by prominent research journals. Even the most respected scholars get rejected now and then. Some of us routinely reject manuscripts as reviewers; occasionally we accept them and almost always ask that revisions be made. At this point, it might be instructive to briefly explicate the underlying principles on which the science of manuscript rejection is based.

Why are research manuscripts rejected? We tell our graduate students (and try to convince ourselves) that to be accepted by any research journal deserving of its eminent editorial board, a manuscript must be based on good theory; assumptions and theoretical bases for hypotheses should be clearly discussed; literature review should be complete, current, and concise; methodology should be sound; evidence for the reliability and validity of measures should be provided; results, interpretations of data, and conclusions should follow from the data analysis and theoretical basis and should be discussed clearly and concisely. All this in ten to fifteen pages of text, plus tables and references. It follows that manuscripts are rejected when they do not fulfill one or more of these requirements.

But there are other reasons manuscripts are rejected. Quite often these reasons are not easily discernible since one has to "read between the lines" and interpret what the reviewers are really saying. Here are a few examples:

1. "This study is atheoretical. Hypotheses do not follow from any logical or theoretical base. Displays an appalling ignorance of important theoretical developments in this area."
   Interpretation: "You are using the wrong theory. See the 1986 Summer issue of this journal for my discussion of the theoretical implications of what you are trying to do."
2. "Incomplete literature review. Recent important work is ignored."
   Interpretation: "See the 1986 Winter issue of this journal for my article on. . . ."
3. "No coherence here. Assumptions and hypotheses go in different directions. Fragmented, disjointed, does not contribute to knowledge in the field."
   Interpretation: "I really don't have the faintest idea what you are talking about."
4. "Methodology is full of holes. No controls. No internal validity."
   Interpretation: "I really don't understand all this mumbo-jumbo."
5. "Analysis is weak. Structural equations do not prove causality. Significance tests are inappropriate."
   Interpretation: "I really don't understand all this mumbo-jumbo."
6. "I am shocked at the total disregard for the welfare of the study's subjects."
   Interpretation: "I tried to do similar things to my Com 101 class but our Protection of Human Subjects Committee wouldn't let me."

Fortunately, research manuscripts in communication are competently reviewed 99.9 percent of the time, and these exogenous reasons for rejection are used infrequently. However, wouldn't it be great if we knew more about the .1 percent of the time when manuscripts are rejected without justification? (If only to allay the suspicion that reviewers are picking on "me.")

I would like to offer the following suggestions to the esteemed editors of our research journals in the interest of dispelling any false impressions about their review procedures (particularly among rejected authors).

1. Discuss and publish criteria used for selecting reviewers. Most journals routinely publish lists of reviewers; this is an excellent practice, but readers and submitters also need to know why they were selected.
2. Publish criteria for accepting articles. This discussion should go beyond the general criteria usually mentioned in "Instructions for Submissions" page and should include the specific instructions that are given to the reviewers.
3. Publish rejection rate for categories of manuscripts.
4. Publish reviewer-agreement coefficients or other appropriate reliability estimates for reviews. A journal is only as good as its editorial board

and/or reviewers. We assume that experts can agree on the merits or demerits of a research manuscript and that a decision to publish or reject is based on this agreement. However, we know very little about the extent to which reviewers of our journals agree on their evaluations of research manuscripts. I hope that agreement is higher than the 30–40 percent rate typically reported by judges of paper competitions for some of our academic organizations. If it isn't, then I wonder if the best research in our field is getting published.

Research: A View from Medill

Margaret T. Gordon

In June 1984, Ed Bassett, the then new dean of the Medill School of Journalism at Northwestern University, announced to the faculty a new organizational structure for the school that included appointing me director of research and inaugurating a new research era at the school. I was surprised because Ed and I had had no previous conversations about the new role or his intentions for it and because I had been granted a leave of absence for the 1984–85 academic year. Nonetheless, I was pleased because for many years—during the deanship of Bill Cole—I had argued (more often than some of my colleagues liked) for more research at Medill.

During the Cole era most of the faculty were not encouraged to do research of the type that would result in scholarly publication. Some were. One outcome was a tension—but not a hostility—between those few faculty who valued being able to engage in research and those who didn't, a tension that tended to parallel beliefs about the degree to which Medill teaching should emphasize the teaching of professional skills relative to "theory" courses designed to teach problem analysis and encourage assessments of the role of the media.

Further, despite the substantial research activity of a *few* faculty, Medill somehow had earned the reputation of having no research activity. And, we had lost accreditation, an action that did not affect applications, enrollments, teaching, the curriculum, or job placements, but that did affect the availability of some research funds. The school was re-accredited in the spring of 1987.

Early in 1985 Arnold Weber, Northwestern University's new president, arrived on campus. By the fall of the year it seemed clear that many of the old rules and norms of our university's politics had changed, and that research activity was going to be much more important than it had been in evaluating individual Medill faculty members (e.g., for tenure and promotion) and for

142

evaluating the school as a whole. It seemed as if perceptions of research output were going to affect power relations among the schools as deans competed for university resources. In short, it was a new ball game. For faculty members who were already engaged in significant research, there was a sense of support they'd never experienced before—and a sense of relief. For those who were hired with no expectation their jobs included research, there was a sense of the rug being pulled out from under them.

Courseloads and expectations for teaching at Medill are high. The nature of the curriculum is such that it requires what observers view as an extraordinary amount of writing by students and, therefore, an extraordinary amount of marking of papers by faculty. Neither students nor faculty are content for papers to be returned with merely a grade, or a grade and a few scribbled comments. Some university administrators have warned us that the curriculum is "too teaching-intensive" to be cost-effective, especially if faculty are to do research as well.

My approach to the research directorship at Medill has been four-pronged. First, I began talking about the need to broaden the definition of what was regarded as "research." Formerly, it seemed to include only social science, historical studies, or legal treatises. Second, I queried the faculty about what they *had been* writing about and what they'd like to work on in the future. The query was accompanied by examples of several types of research.

- Research directly tied to teaching (e.g., market surveys and public opinion polling)
- Research about the media industry (e.g., concentration of ownership, computerization of newsrooms)
- Research industry spokespersons say would be useful in
  - Advertising (e.g., how are product images and sales related to television and newspaper advertising?)
  - Circulation (e.g., what model predicts sellouts and returns from vendors in order to minimize returns?)
  - Editorial (e.g., what can be done to enhance credibility?)
- Research about the media and public policy (e.g., should news personnel have had access to all information about the Grenada invasion?)
- Social science research (e.g., measuring the impacts of investigative reports)
- Legal research (e.g., laws governing satellite communications)
- Historical research (e.g., history of the "standards and practices" offices of the networks as gatekeepers and shapers of American culture)

I also asked about the principles published in a statement written by a joint committee of the American Society of Newspaper Editors (ASNE) and Association for Education in Journalism and Mass Communication (AEJMC) known as the CONEE (Committee on News and Editorial Education) statement, especially relevant to faculty hired primarily because of their professional records and less likely to do research publishable in traditional scholarly journals.

Third, I began working with individual faculty members in developing research and/or writing plans and objectives.

And fourth, we have begun a series of informal seminars sharing interests, ideas, and plans.

What I want to share with you is that Medill has had a lot of "closet" researchers, and now the enthusiasm for scholarly work is spreading. People are even discovering they share interests they didn't know they had in common! A new endowment for a research professorship only adds to the excitement.

There are full-fledged or nascent projects on such varied topics as:

- professionalism and the profit motive
- ethics and professionalism
- media coverage of the underclass
- media and missing children
- how a story on a topic turns into a media fad or trend
- mass communications law, technology, and change
- development of creative strategies
- trends in business reporting and business sections
- a review of findings from thirteen "news room study projects," each of which has involved community surveys, content analyses, and interviews with local editors and reporters
- the disappearing mass audience related to the new technologies and segmentation of markets

Now my job is to spread the word, to change Medill's image from one that included no research to one that retains a primary emphasis on professional training but now also includes a wide range of research activities that already is contributing to the scholarly community and the profession.

Organizing and Planning for Research

Ed Mullins

O ne of the longest-running controversies in social science asks a decep-
tively simple question: How do you best bring about effective reform —
by changing institutions or changing attitudes? This is clearly a chicken-and-egg
argument. Since chickens and eggs are both here, the pragmatist would simply
observe that they are both needed to sustain the poultry business. Similarly,
institutional change and attitudinal change are both needed to change undesir-
able behavior and then to sustain desirable behavior in groups and individuals.

At the University of Alabama, we have worked for ten years on institutional, attitudinal, and behavioral change in the mission, goals, and objectives
of the School of Communication. In 1978, under the leadership of then Dean
William H. Melson, we began systematic strategic and annual planning. This
kind of self-conscious planning was unheard of in mass communication education at the time. Now it is an accepted article of faith for at least half of the
more than three hundred mass communication units in the United States, and
even those not doing it are talking about it.

Emerging from our planning efforts were goals to start a Ph.D. program
and to organize and develop a research program. The two goals, of course,
were not unrelated. It did not require great vision to see that the top research
programs on our campus and elsewhere existed in units with strong doctoral
programs.

Another major goal was the systematic recruitment of a research-trained
faculty. We needed individuals whose enthusiasm for research would rub off
on the current faculty.

While a Ph.D. program would help in our research objectives, we knew
it would take longer to get into the Ph.D. game than the research game. We
simply did not have the faculty breadth and depth to launch a quality doctoral program in 1978. We were also in the midst of unprecedented growth.

From four hundred students in 1973, we soared to sixteen hundred by 1978 and were still at that level in 1987. Teaching loads were already heavy. A doctoral program would just make matters worse.

While making research basic to our mission, at the same time we vowed not to let other basics slide. That meant devoting as much time, or more, to building quality in our undergraduate courses, especially in the skills courses so important to practitioners.

The development of our research program had these major thrusts:

1. To establish new faculty positions and to recruit new faculty members with research training. That meant hiring people with the Ph.D. In 1976, seven of seventeen, or 41 percent of the faculty had the doctoral degree. By 1987, it was 75 percent, thirty of forty. Basically a skills-oriented undergraduate unit, the school received no criticism of its plans from key professional constituencies. We invited them to our school as part of our Professional-in-Residence program and organized active alumni and other support groups, including a board of visitors representing national media interests. When we submitted and received approval of our Ph.D. proposal in 1986, members of the sixteen-member board wrote letters endorsing the program. Several have pledged scholarship support for our first doctoral students.

2. To establish and equip a research and service center that would contain a survey research unit and a media institute for continuing education. Acceptance and use of our communication Research and Service Center have exceeded our expectations. More than 200 surveys, the majority of them sponsored, have been conducted since the Capstone Poll began in 1980, making it the leading academic polling unit in the region. A collaborative effort with the Department of Political Science, the poll is also the national headquarters for the Network of State Polls. More than fifty well-attended workshops, conferences, and short courses have been conducted under the auspices of the Alabama Media Institute, which is patterned after the American Press Institute. The center's equipment includes six Apple microcomputers; two Televideo terminals connected to the university's mainframe computer and to a word-processing and data-processing network within the academic departments; dot-matrix, letter-quality, and laser printers; and a microfilm reader.

The center oversees a mini-grant competitive research program funded out of its operating budget. Profits from surveys are used to buy equipment.

Eighteen permanent telephone stations are used to conduct surveys. The poll is connected to the mainframe computer for processing current and archival poll data. Co-directors of the poll are our research director and a political science faculty member. This marriage was made in research heaven and continues uninterrupted after seven years. Regular news releases are sent out on public-issue polls. The co-directors have just completed a book on the 1986

Alabama gubernatorial election campaign. Using data from polls conducted for the state's largest newspaper, the *Birmingham News*, the authors explain what led to the election of the state's first Republican governor since Reconstruction. It was quite a story, and we were involved from both a journalistic and research viewpoint.

The biggest problem we now face in the research center is how to meet all legitimate requests by our faculty and outsiders. The center has a secretary, an assistant director, two permanently assigned research assistants, and occasional project-related part-time help—but this falls short of our needs.

3. To require strict accountability by faculty for release time to conduct research. In 1976 average faculty loads were almost four courses per semester. Today the average load is just over 2.5 courses per semester. Under exceptional circumstances—which means high quality research plans submitted by a faculty member with a reliable track record—we will reduce course loads to two and one (two courses for one semester and one course for the second). Research plans are proposed and reviewed annually. Reduced workloads for researchers are continued if the department head and dean find the productivity acceptable. No fixed quantitative measures of this productivity are used. It is based on the informed judgment of the department head and dean, who frequently must check with colleagues about the value of a particular effort. A large part of a faculty's merit pay increase is tied to research productivity.

How has it all worked out?

One measure is how often I must write memos acknowledging new publications. Since becoming dean in 1983, I have assumed the responsibility for school publicity—both internal and external. I want to recognize the producers. No month passes when I don't write several memos about a new article, paper, book, or other scholarly achievement of our faculty. In sheer quantitative terms, holding the number of faculty constant, our research productivity has increased four-fold in ten years. Of eleven divisions on campus, only Arts and Sciences and Engineering produced more publications in 1985–86 per full-time faculty than the School of Communication.

Is it any good? Does it matter? If outside recognition is a measure of quality, our efforts have been good and they do matter. One faculty member was selected as the university's Outstanding Young Scholar. Three have been named editors of national research and/or commentary journals. A dozen are on editorial review boards. We have received an endowed chair worth nearly one million dollars, and the first holder has produced a monograph on telecommunications regulation just published by Longman's Press. We have received a forty-thousand-dollar research endowment from a public utility in the state. Several of our faculty are engaged in major funded consultations and research projects.

If I said that all this happened without problems, I would not be telling the truth. Some faculty are still doing no research, but at least no one is hostile to research. Some faculty who came to us with great promise and who received favorable schedules in the beginning to allow for research have failed to produce. They have moved on. But these are in the minority.

Our efforts have been greatly helped by a central administration that bought in to our plans as part of an overall quest for quality. Now funds are slowing. Our next challenge will be to do more with less and to be more aggressive in pursuit of outside funding.

But the essence of productivity is doing more with less, and we will look again at our systems and our people and do what it takes to keep the momentum going.

Bring on those Ph.D. students.

The Uncertain Connection between Academia and Newspapers

ALBERT E. GOLLIN

The field of communications research is very active these days, judging by a number of indicators: the proliferation of professional journals; conferences that take stock and contribute to intellectual conviviality; and books, textbooks, and yearbooks that package ideas and research results. Yet, despite all this activity, there are few signs of bridges that link people in media organizations with academically-based researchers. My experience is restricted to the newspaper world, but I believe that a similar sense of separation and marginality characterizes the relationship between communication scholars and media professionals in broadcasting as well.

There are, of course, networks linking journalism educators and future employers of their students around issues of accreditation. The shared interests of advertising and marketing professors and the newspaper world have been an active concern of the International Newspaper Advertising and Marketing Executives (INAME), the American Newspaper Publishers Association (ANPA), and the Newspaper Advertising Bureau (NAB) for some time, and the traffic among these sectors has been growing to their mutual advantage. But what is missing is a lively interplay between communication researchers in journalism schools (or other academic departments) and newspaper people who seek or might benefit from research on issues of mutual concern. Few editors, reporters, or newspaper executives regularly read *Journalism Quarterly* or other journalism research outlets. And one wonders how influential are the industry issues raised in *Editor & Publisher* or *presstime* on the agendas of communications researchers compared with the intellectual trends and currents that ripple through the Association for Education in Journalism and Mass Communication (AEJMC) or other academically-based associations.

It is possible that the short-term applied needs of mass media organizations and the longer-range interests of academics are fundamentally mismatched, hindering the possibilities for fruitful exchange. Timetables for getting things done differ considerably, as does the capacity to organize research quickly, gather and analyze data, and write or present results in an actionable context. These and other institutional contrasts certainly can have limited possibilities for collaboration. But developments *within* the newspaper business, I suggest, have had a more direct bearing upon the current situation.

Foremost among these has been the steady growth in the number and professionalism of researchers working in newspapers and newspaper associations (including NAB). The Newspaper Research Council (NRC), which began more than twenty years ago as a small group of advisors to the NAB's research program, incorporated itself in 1977 and currently has more than two hundred members. These researchers are primarily engaged in local marketing studies, but they are increasingly involved in editorial research (surveys and content studies) and in managing the work of research consulting firms on behalf of their newspapers. The NRC holds twice-yearly meetings lasting three days during which research presentations are made that add substantially to the skills and knowledge of the membership.

Another key factor has been a concomitant growth in the demand for the services of professional research consulting firms. Originally, beginning in the 1930s, firms such as Belden Associates (San Antonio, Texas) conducted periodic market studies for individual client newspapers. Now, alongside dozens of smaller firms that regularly service individual newspapers, one can point to Simmons Market Research Bureau, Scarborough, and Windsor Systems as suppliers of research and marketing information on a large scale, doing both syndicated and custom studies on a year-round basis. By one recent estimate, the total amount spent on newspaper-sponsored research of all types exceeded fifty million dollars. Little or none of this was spent to support academic media or communication research, although a few moonlighting academics have gained a reputation as consultants to individual newspapers or chains.

What occurred, I suggest, is that newspapers hired staff or consultants on a proprietary basis to conduct research that came increasingly to be seen as necessary to deal with their changing marketing situation or to meet certain organizational requirements. Academic research resources were, by comparison, limited, scattered, and lacking in demonstrated follow-through. The same trend was observable in the shift on the part of the federal government away from reliance upon academic research organizations to meet their policy and programmatic research needs toward social and policy research firms able to respond rapidly and to maintain continuity in their contacts with sponsoring agencies. As potential providers of research and problem-solving help, therefore, academic researchers simply could not offer credible competition.

These developments were nowhere better illustrated than in the conduct of research during the brief history of the Newspaper Readership Project. Initiated by the boards of ANPA and NAB in 1977, it was carried out with the participation of sixteen newspaper associations for six years, concluding its activities in 1983. In that period more than 800 newspapers contributed nearly $5 million; $1.5 million of these funds were spent on a wide-ranging research program that touched on all aspects of circulation and readership issues. In all, forty studies of varying scope were mounted, yielding more than eighty reports oriented to the concerns of editors, publishers, and circulation and marketing managers. It was an unprecedented effort conducted by and for the newspaper business—a significant departure from the marketing research aimed at advertisers that had long been part of newspaper sales promotion activities. Academic researchers played almost no part in the Readership Project's activities.

Diagnosis and problem-solving were the twin objectives of this sustained program of applied research. Dissemination of findings was achieved by presentations at major industry meetings, workshops (including ten regional research workshops for editors), and by the distribution of more than 30,000 copies of research reports. Although this was done primarily through industry channels, copies of these reports have been made available to journalism researchers and educators. In addition, many of the results were summarized in Leo Bogart's book, *Press and Public* (Hillsdale, N.J.: Lawrence Erlbaum, 1981).

One aspect of the Readership Project did contribute to bridge-building between the industry and journalism researchers. Its financial support for the ANPA News Research Center, under the direction of Max McCombs (then at Syracuse University), was instrumental in the preparation of thirty-nine brief reports of research mainly by academic communications scholars on applications of small-scale studies they had conducted or supervised. But with the demise of the Readership Project, this ANPA activity was terminated, thus ending a collaborative effort that stretched back to 1966, when the first "News Research for Better Newspapers" was published by ANPA under the direction first of Chilton Bush (Stanford University) and then of Galen Rarick (Ohio State University).

Is there any role for academic research centers in light of this unpromising history? The answer to this question can take either of two contrasting forms. One is the development of testable conceptions of the mass media and their interrelations in a societal context that can illuminate the situation and choices confronting media organizations. Newspapers need to draw upon challenging strategic concepts as well as "tactical" information that guides concrete decisions, especially realistic assessments of changing relationships between the mass media and society as reflected in audience habits and preferences. The other is to seek opportunities among mid-size and smaller newspapers, which typically have more limited resources to sponsor the kinds of research or organizational consulting they might need. It will take patience on the part of both parties and a willingness to learn the "folkways" of the other, given the contrasting institutional imperatives noted earlier. But collaborative ventures can provide a variety of benefits to faculty and students while allowing newspapers to gain access to expertise whose cumulative contributions can help them serve their readers better.

Why Aren't the Practitioners Interested?

Mark R. Levy

L ike workers in other industries, we communication researchers often view the world from the vantage point of our professional and disciplinary fortresses. We would like to believe that others share our intense interest in our research topics and discoveries. And many of us would like to believe that our work is of some long-run practical importance. Unfortunately, however, even the most charitable reading of history suggests that too often communications practitioners are not interested in what we have to say. Our research and our theories just don't matter to them; our work is fundamentally irrelevant.

Let me expand on this gloomy assessment by sharing a recent research experience. For several years now, my colleagues and I have been studying the public's awareness and comprehension of the news—in short, what people learn and don't learn from reading and watching the news. Although most of that research has focused on the mass media audience, we have always thought that our work had important implications for the practices and policies of the news professions, especially TV news. Indeed, we have tried both to involve working journalists in our research and to make our findings available to those who "make" the news.

To say that our studies have been greeted with less than total enthusiasm by even the most responsible and self-aware members of the journalistic community is to understate our frustration. Some journalists have shown a passing interest in what we and others have learned in this area. But many have reacted with hostility, or worse yet, indifference.

It is not merely a case of hurt feelings or academic hubris that fuels our frustration. After all, the competitive and economic pressures facing journalists

This essay draws on materials presented in John Robinson and Mark Levy, *The Main Source: Learning From Television News* (Newbury Park, Calif.: Sage Publications, 1986).

are severe. Entrenched newswork practices and long-held professional ideologies *seem* to get the job done. The time and rewards required for "philosophical" or "theoretical" discussions about the obligation of journalists to inform a democratic citizenry are in very short supply in most newsrooms. Still, as a matter of common sense and philosophical preference, we believe that journalists could be more effective communicators if they were aware of, understood and applied the findings of news comprehensions research.

In taking our case to the working press, we usually make the following arguments:

1. Normative theories of the press require journalists to inform the public, not just make information public;
2. Informing the public requires some fundamental changes in the way journalists work; but few, if any, of those changes represent a threat to professional autonomy;
3. Journalism might be a less alienating and professionally more rewarding career if journalists were more self-conscious about how much of the news was "getting through" to the audience—and if journalists could point to examples in their work where increased public awareness made a difference in people's lives;
4. News that informed as it "told" might in the long-run actually attract larger and more enthusiastic audiences—no small consideration for a media system based on competition and enterprise.

We have made this pitch on numerous occasions, in newsrooms in the United States and England, even to news organizations that were paying us for advice. Our work, based as it is on strong scientific evidence, democratic theory, and enlightened self-interest poses an enormous challenge to the practicing journalist. So far, that challenge has gone unmet.

Do We Have a Research Future Together?
It Sure Hasn't Been Much of a Past!

Alex S. Edelstein

The question before the House is whether the media and the schools can do research together. Well, to answer the question partially, it hasn't honestly been much of a past!

I remember a study conducted many years ago by Professor Jean Kerrick of the University of California. It asserted that editorial writers who were opposed to a point of view nonetheless did a more thorough job of arguing the case than those who actually favored the position. Never mind the high-minded spirit of public service that guides an editorial writer in such circumstances (an imperative often imposed by a publisher or an editorial board at election time), just ask yourself what we should know about people who are subjected to these and other pressures in the newsroom or in editorial offices. The schools have done research that touches upon situations of that kind, but few of the media feel they need it, and even fewer have bought it.

I remember my exposure to research at Stanford as a master's student who wondered naively when the faculty were going to talk about journalism. They did, of course. But Chick Bush, the director, also got us involved in his Hometown Newspaper Readership studies, which were forbears of a sort of "precision" journalism. We interviewed readers and studied the results for individual papers and cumulatively for classes of newspapers, and, in the process, learned a lot about journalism.

Last week the publisher of a daily newspaper visited us and told us that his readership studies were proprietary and he could not even discuss the results with us. We had made a pitch to his research director to do them, but we were not taken very seriously. We didn't offer enough security (as the Soviets observed of Los Angeles?), perhaps? Too slow a turnaround time, perhaps? More credibility from big name commercial companies (from Texas), perhaps?

Let's dismiss our doubts for a moment and try an idea, one that has a limited history, unfortunately, but has enjoyed some degree of success. What if newspapers—regionally, let's say—were to help establish and nurture first-rate media research institutes in a leading school in their area? That would build prestige for the institute, the newspapers would get better research, and they would get more of it for the money. They would have readily accessible to them valuable data banks that could answer 1,001 questions. They would advance their field and their own enterprise at the same time. But as intelligent a step as this would be, it has occurred rarely and is not likely to occur again. Right now another daily newspaper with which I'm familiar is doing some polls on various problems and issues that might well be done in a first-rate media institute, but they prefer a commercial pollster for reasons that they would not share with us. It's difficult to conceive of the talent at the university producing any less a product than the newspaper has in hand.

Speaking in less intimate and more general terms, I can remember Chick Bush saying, "it's no trick to ask questions, but it's quite a trick to ask the right questions." To illustrate briefly, I have followed with interest recent concerns expressed by the media about their "image." There has been great disputation about credibility and more recently about ethics. About fifteen years ago I challenged Roper's findings that heralded the astonishing supremacy of television in news and its greater credibility as a medium. The Television Information Office ultimately conceded that by asking different questions one got different answers. It turned out that if the news event were very important to the individual then that person read newspapers more; for the usual news menu, however, television was adequate and even offered bonuses in sight, sound, and ease of effort. But practically no one volunteered any statements about credibility. Locally I encountered yawns and skepticism as to the importance of what I had found. But a blurb in *Editor & Publisher* rang the phone off the hook, and I was brought to New York to regale the American Newspaper Publishers Association (ANPA). There followed a research grant and a pat on the back from their News Research Center.

The lessons are obvious. Nothing venal, but local media don't take their own schools seriously, nor do they cultivate the research faculty, no matter how strong their national reputations. The reasons may be found in the nature of the newspaper and its editors. They put out a product every day, have a tiger by the tail in the newsroom and out of it, and are reflections of their activities—short range and self-absorbed. We could make all kinds of time for them, but they really have no time for us.

More recently the media have become more sharply conscious of the concept of ethics. It doesn't do a lot of good to tell them that their audiences may not be thinking in terms of ethics but something a little more obvious—

let's call it comportment. The way in which the media invariably address their sources, adversarially, and the way they serve as observers and outsiders with respect to most events forces them to intrude themselves to do their jobs. This has a great deal more to do with public attitudes toward them than any self-flatulent thing called ethics. It should be understood that ethics represents professional conduct and assumes that the professional controls his or her own environment. Why pretend that the media really can do this? One only gets caught up in one's own disguise. A good media research institute would look into this and related questions and help the media solve their identity crisis.

I have heard many media people say that they can't abide *Journalism Quarterly*; the fact is, no doubt, that while they may curse *JQ* they ignore *Journalism Educator*. Media people have not prepared themselves to read *JQ* in the same way as their specialized reporters have prepared themselves to read journals in the physical sciences. Specialized reporters in those areas do not carp at the inevitable jargon associated with a scientific activity. New words are needed to classify and explain new phenomena. A media research institute could review journalism research and cull from it some useful knowledge, and it could stage seminars for the media that would bring fresh ideas to bear on their constant concerns.

We have from time to time collaborated with the media on programs involving advanced training of undergraduates, career enhancement programs for working newspeople, and celebratory programs on a variety of topics relating to freedom of information. We have staged innumerable visits by distinguished journalists. Many of our very able faculty have done research for the media, but each project has been limited in scope and could be compared to a seized opportunity in terms of time and place. Each activity came about because of our initiative rather than that of the newspapers, and each activity, however successful, quickly was forgotten. There was no institutional memory, for we (the schools and the media) had built no institutions.

It is possible that such ad hoc experiences may strike some readers as representing more than a modicum of success; it is more success, perhaps, than a hundred other schools might be able to report. But in my view it has produced only limited rewards, gained on each occasion by disproportionate effort, and lived only a short life. Only a two-way commitment to an institutional relationship offers promise of meaningful interdependence and success. Anything short of that will doom us to continued impotence.

The Fault Is in Ourselves

BRIAN WINSTON

The hostility of media personnel to the work of mass communications scholars was noted early. By 1941 Paul Lazarsfeld was already arguing that the
mass media were overly sensitive to "the criticism of intellectuals": but Lazarsfeld was able to comment then that, despite this hostility, "actually most publishers and broadcasters have been very generous and cooperative."[1]

Seven years later, the lines had hardened. Addressing a conference on communications research in 1948, Lazarsfeld began what was to be described as
a "provocative speech." "If there is any one institutional disease to which the
media of mass communications seem particularly subject," he said, "it is a nervous reaction to criticism. As a student of mass media I have been continually struck and occasionally puzzled by this reaction, for it is the media themselves which so vigorously defend the principles guaranteeing the right to
criticise."[2]

The situation today remains as Lazarsfeld described it. My own content
analysis work with the Glasgow University Media Group provoked a reaction from British broadcast journalists that has continued for years. Recently,
the United Kingdom commercial news organization (ITN) allowed an academic full access to the scripts of the programs analyzed by us a decade earlier. His findings, published last year, were that we had manipulated the evidence, claiming, for instance, statements to have been made on camera that
had not in fact been said. We, of course, still stand by our original analysis,
and my colleagues at Glasgow still have the video cassettes to prove these
points. That an organization as culturally powerful as ITN should still be pursuing a small group of academics for what was said about its work in books
published in 1976 and 1980 bespeaks something nearer a pathology than a
"nervous reaction."

The Glasgow case is admittedly extreme since the analysis in those books revealed a failure on the part of the news organization to obey the law of the land, viz, a requirement of the Television Act that the news be balanced and impartial. That our group was arguing for the law to be changed, because the requirement could never be met, was not—and has not been—noticed by the professionals.

The fault in the relationship, however, is not entirely one-sided. Sensitivity apart, the media professionals have been led to expect results from the research community that have been largely undelivered and that, if proper academic integrity is to be maintained, should perhaps never have been promised.

Lazarsfeld, again, is emblematic here. He says that "there ought to be a way of making criticism more useful and manageable for those who offer it and those who receive it."[3]

Arguably this was the goal conditioning his entire output as a scholar. However, such an agenda is not immediately within the fundamental traditions of the academy. It is not so much that the Lazarsfeld goal fails to mesh with the ideal of fearless intellectual inquiry but rather that it sends the wrong signal to both those offering and those receiving criticism. It proposes an ameliorative function for academic work to the exclusion of all else.

The brief and vexed relationship of Lazarsfeld to the critical theorist Theodor W. Adorno illustrates the dangers of Lazarsfeld's position. In Todd Gitlin's account,[4] Adorno found the institutional framework that Lazarsfeld had created extremely restrictive intellectually. At this time (1938) Lazarsfeld had established the Princeton Project, and it was here that he sought to accommodate Adorno. But, as Adorno was to write, "there appeared to be little room for critical social research in the framework of the Princeton Project. Its charter, which came from the Rockefeller Foundation, expressly stipulated that the investigations must be performed within the limits of the commercial radio system prevailing in the United States."[5] Subsequently, Lazarsfeld was to establish an even more direct relationship with the media via the good offices of Frank Stanton, the social psychologist who rose to the presidency of CBS. From Adorno's perspective (and it is one shared by many European scholars, even those who are not of his particular political persuasion) this relationship was to prove somewhat unhealthy for the growth of mass communication studies in the United States.

The irony is that this willingness to accommodate the industries did not produce the utilitarian research Lazarsfeld had promised. Certainly the research tradition has given the media neither irrefutable scientific truths needed to rebut charges of improper influence nor incontrovertible data to support claims of media power.

In short, the ameliorative agenda failed to ameliorate. And the very attempt to make such an agenda central to the academic project led the media to believe that the academy would always behave in a supportive fashion. The sensitivity of the media to academic criticism was thus exacerbated. The academy was not expected to offer less than positive research results or take oppositional theoretical positions. When academics dared to do these things, the sense of betrayal in some sections of the media was acute.

The final twist here is that the negative research was often close, methodologically, to the industry's own research work. Indeed, some academic research techniques are industrial in origin.

It is this history that causes me to reach the conclusion that the desire for industrial relevance on the part of academics is misplaced. The tradition of unfettered critical inquiry should be pursued. There is no reason why academic investigation should be in any way directly useful to practitioners, and there is no reason for academics to seek the attention of professionals.

It would be better for the results of academic inquiry to inform the teaching of media practices at all levels. In such teaching, students should be forced to confront the conflicts between professionals and academics. In this way, one hopes such students will develop into a generation of media professionals able to rise above the nervous reactions of their predecessors—able, in fact, to use the work of the academy whether or not it was specifically designed for them.

Notes

1. Paul F. Lazarsfeld, "An Episode in the History of Social Research: A Memoir," in Donald Fleming and Bernard Bailyn, eds., *The Intellectual Migration: Europe and America, 1930–1960* (Cambridge, Mass.: Harvard University Press, 1969), quoted in Todd Gitlin, "Media Sociology: The Dominant Paradigm," *Theory and Society* 6 (September 1978): 232.

2. Paul F. Lazarsfeld, "The Role of Criticism in the Management of Mass Media," *Journalism Quarterly* 25 (June 1948): 115.

3. Ibid.

4. Gitlin, "Media Sociology," passim.

5. Theodor W. Adorno, "Scientific Experiences of a European Scholar in America," in Fleming and Bailyn, eds., *The Intellectual Migration*, as quoted in Gitlin, "Media Sociology," 229.

Mass Communication Researchers and Massive Obfuscation

Gerald Stone

ESCHEW OBFUSCATION was a little sign a faculty colleague tacked to his office door. The call for clarity warned journalism students to "avoid confusing" readers.

I've often wondered why conferring a Ph.D. in journalism or mass communication relegates us to a life of pedantic writing. Resumés of freshly minted Ph.D.s in our field prove most have extensive experience in journalism-related occupations. They made their living writing. They will teach writing to undergraduate journalism students—and they will teach well. But when it comes to writing a research report, Ph.D.s obfuscate to beat the band.

I agree with this volume's authors that the mass communication industry pays far too little attention to research. A wealth of information exists, but it gets little use. I agree that a lot of industry practitioners are quick to cast aspersions about the quality of research when, in fact, they are not interested enough to find out what's there.

But I think researchers are at least equally guilty. Much of our work is almost unintelligible to any audience except other Ph.D.s—and often only those Ph.D.s whose research background is in the same specialty area.

Journalism and mass communication researchers are not the only obtuse writers. Sociologist Mark Oromaner offered a particularly critical assessment in a 1979 article based on a study of citations. He reported that faculty members generally said that an almost insignificant portion of published research in their respective fields was worthy of appearing in print, much less of being read or cited.[1] But the pervasiveness of writing academic gobbledygook is no excuse, particularly for people who know how to write.

What happens? Why do former journalists write research incomprehensibly? I have a few pet theories about what happens and what improvements might be made.

161

1. We are taught to be precise in our scientific writing. So we use jargon such as "salient," "factor analysis with oblique rotation," "cognitive space," and "positive canonical loadings." Footnotes aren't good enough; we include this jargon in the text. Mind you, we're not showing off; we are just being precise, as we've been taught.

While we instruct our students not to use words their audiences won't understand, we break that rule in virtually every research article. We persist in writing only for our scholarly colleagues.

As editor of *Newspaper Research Journal* (*NRJ*), I see an incredible amount of jargon in submitted articles. Many pass review because they deal with interesting and current topics of practical value to the newspaper industry. But, reviewers often say the piece needs a "heavy edit for readability."

To show how to write research for lay audiences of industry practitioners, I mailed these authors copies of Phil Meyer's 1980 *NRJ* article on national versus local news. Two paragraphs were highlighted in which Meyer explained multiple regression analysis in terms of how inches of snowfall might affect newspaper street sales.[2] A seventh grader could understand it. Few people write about research as clearly as Meyer, but too many mass communications researchers never even think to try.

2. Symptomatic of the jargon problem is the use of tables in research articles. Tables contain far too much detail and needless numerical clutter. A table should offer the reader a quick overview of the research data. Instead, we report that 59.83 percent of a sample read editorials the average length of which was 11.357 column inches. Why not report that 60 percent read the 11-inch editorials? Approximations should be sufficient; certainly they are more easily grasped and remembered. If the one hundredth place percentages seem cumbersome, how must a reported F value, eigenvalue, or beta weight seem to the uninitiated? Or don't we care?

3. Our choice of problems to research is often misguided. We know the industry isn't reading our work, but we continue to provide extensive reports about the correlation between watching MTV and reading the comics section of the newspaper. (That research example is more useful than many we choose.) Our decision of topics to investigate is influenced more by the topics our colleagues write about in the journals than our own knowledge of what is either important or needed.

4. We write for our academic colleagues as if using some secret fraternity handshake: "Of course, no one would refute Brown and Jones (1968, 1972) whose landmark work was replicated by Williams (1975; see also Smith, 1978) with findings surpassed only by Davis (1982) and Thomas (1985). The implications are obvious."

Obviously, the implications are a complete mystery unless you've been reading Brown, Williams, Davis, *et al.*, or unless you look up the sources. Isn't that a bit much to ask of the reader? Why not summarize the points these authors made, relevant to the current topic? If they aren't relevant, leave them out.

5. We don't explain our findings properly. I have read brilliantly planned and executed research studies that never quite mentioned the outcomes. Regardless of whether the findings supported the hypothesis, destroyed the hypothesis, or offered conflicting outcomes, the authors just didn't bother to tell readers what was found or what it might mean.

6. One of the worst faults researchers have is not providing conclusions and recommendations. We are quick to say more study is needed or to point the way for future research (both are appropriate), but often we don't bother to tell readers why our research was important or what can be done with the findings.

Consider the commercial newspaper consultant who does a three-year followup readership study and finds a 12 percent drop in the number of young-adult readers. The consultant tells the publisher: "You've got a big problem among your young-adult readers. Let's look at their content preferences to see if we can reverse the trend."

Academic researchers often are too cautious about making recommendations. If we find a + .92 correlation between size of the front page topfold picture and people's preference for selecting that paper, we're likely to report that people seem to prefer larger pictures. We neglect to suggest street sales will improve if the topfold front page picture is larger than those in competing papers.

The same is true for more basic research topics. These investigations are rich lodes, but we don't bother to relate them to real-world applications. Do we think these applications are self-evident? I contend we don't think far enough beyond our findings. Hence, we miss the opportunity to suggest applications, which is another responsibility of research writers.

If we want to increase the value of mass communication research, we must remember we are not writing just for our Ph.D. research colleagues. If we are to add to the body of new information in our field, we must do a better job communicating that knowledge in our research writing.

We do no service to the field when we use the Ph.D. as a license to obfuscate.

Notes

1. Mark Oromaner, "When Publications Perish," *Scholarly Publishing* 10 (July 1979): 339–44.

2. Philip Meyer, "The National vs. Local News Controversy: A Behavioral Approach," *Newspaper Research Journal* 1 (February 1980), 3–10.

A Lesson We Teach about Research

Guido H. Stempel III

When we, as communications faculty, express concern about the way editors ignore research, we need to recognize that many of them are our graduates and that they have learned well a lesson we have taught them. By our example, we have said to them that research is not very important, and unfortunately they have taken our word for it.

How have we taught them this? Simply by our curricula. When a student sees that several courses in writing and reporting plus courses in editing, journalism history, communication law, and media ethics are the requirements, he or she gets the message. Research isn't on that list. It isn't important.

Some journalism programs offer research to undergraduate students, and a very few make it a requirement or an alternate requirement. For the most part, though, we see research courses as something reserved for the graduate program. That, too, tells the undergraduate student that it's not something vital to the working journalist.

Now this might not be much of a problem if we worked research findings into appropriate places in other courses, but the evidence that we do that is not strong.

There is perhaps an exception that proves the rule in that regard. When Bruce Westley revised his *News Editing* (Boston: Houghton Mifflin, 1972) in the early 1970s, he made a monumental effort to get pertinent research findings into the book. This was not a matter of having a chapter on research, as some have done, but rather a matter of spotting research findings where they belonged throughout the entire book. The problem is that his example has not been widely followed in texts for basic skills courses.

The unfortunate result of this neglect is that we have abandoned the field to market researchers. Now there's nothing wrong with market research, except that it can take you only so far. Eventually you have to deal with improving the product. The market researcher may not be much help at this point because his or her background is likely to be in marketing or business administration. His or her knowledge of editorial journalism may be very limited.

It is because of this that I feel the media today are in the same position that the American auto industry was in the mid-1970s. While our auto industry was preoccupied with marketing, their Japanese competitors were perfecting front-wheel drive. The result is well known.

However, I'm not sure that the media got the right message from that situation. They have made a folk hero out of Lee Iacocca, the marketer *par excellence*. I wonder, however, how many people would have read Iacocca's best-selling autobiography if Chrysler engineers hadn't figured out front-wheel drive in the late 1970s.

It is important for editors and program managers to know that they don't really know what their readers want and that a better product is possible. It is also important that they recognize that research offers better answers on both scores.

Those of us in journalism education must make our students more aware of the importance of research. In part, this must be done teacher by teacher and school by school. However, some bigger moves are needed as well. One would be for journalism accrediting to put some emphasis on the place of research in the curriculum. My experience with three previsit reports I helped prepare leaves me with the feeling that there is no expectation that research should be in the undergraduate curriculum.

A second move would be for this question to work its way into the program of the annual convention of the Association for Education in Journalism and Mass Communication. There is a research emphasis in the program now, but it is rarely directed toward the undergraduate curriculum. The convention offers the best opportunity to get the issue before large numbers of journalism teachers.

Finally, it will help if the media will look more to journalism schools for help with research projects. This would be mutually beneficial. Journalism faculty members can help the media improve their offerings. The media can help faculty members make research a more viable part of the undergraduate curriculum.

Communication Research and the Practice of Journalism

ARNOLD H. ISMACH

The *New Yorker*, in a brief essay in its Talk of the Town column on July 15, 1985, decried what it viewed as the triumph of commerce over merit in the mass media. In book publishing, in television (and presumably in other commercial media), the essayist complained, content decisions were dictated by marketplace considerations. That marketing orientation, the author suggested, eroded the viability of the "marketplace of ideas" concept that had long buttressed American support for free speech and press:

> In classical political theory, the marketplace was a forum in which anyone who had anything on his mind could express it. According to this theory, the chain of events by which the public found out about the world began with the individual person looking out upon the world and reflecting on what he saw; then, perhaps after much labor, the person brought the product of his thought to the marketplace, there to be displayed with the work of others; and then the public picked and chose what it liked. But in the new system the ends of the chain have been joined to form a closed loop. The individual, instead of looking out upon the world, looks out upon public opinion, trying to find what the public would like to hear. Then he tries his best to duplicate that, and brings his finished product into a marketplace in which others are competing to do the same. The public, turning to our culture to find out about the world, discovers there nothing but its own reflection. The unexamined world, meanwhile, drifts blind into the future.

A bleaker assessment of the marriage of audience research and media content would be hard to find. The *New Yorker* piece was focused on television entertainment programming and book publishing, but its argument would apply equally to movies, magazines, newspapers, and broadcast journalism. We are living in the Information Society, and the organizing principle for that society is research.

Many in journalism also bemoan audience research, which they regard as an unwelcome intruder in the newsroom. They view it as a violation of their decision-making turf, a threat to their independence, the substitution of cash-register values for professional news judgment. The increased use of audience research in the newspaper business during the 1970s was scathingly described in journals and trade magazines as "supermarketing" the news, a cynical attempt to sell readers what they wanted instead of what they needed. Similar, if milder, reactions followed the widespread adoption of audience research by television news consultants a decade earlier.

The apparent assumption by critics, internal and external, is that the study of communication behavior and its application to news is necessarily corrupting, that mere knowledge of how and when and why people use information will lead to manipulation (much as the advertiser or the politician attempts to use communication theory to sway audiences), and that the application of communication theory to the practice of journalism will necessarily lead to media products bereft of substance.

The only problem with those widely held assumptions is that they are uniformly wrong. Although there is abundant evidence that some research-based change has found its way into the mainstream of newspaper practice (expanded coverage of subjects such as health is an example), most journalists are oblivious to research and negative toward anything that smacks of marketing. Newspaper research directors are in a position to judge that assertion. Privately, some of them complain that despite compelling data that call for changes in news practices, editors and writers choose to ignore them.

A number of possible reasons come to mind in trying to explain journalists' disdain for research. One is a belief that the available research is invalid or in some other way inadequate and that journalists know this. Other explanations are more plausible:

- Research findings are inaccessible. They appear in publications that most journalists don't monitor.
- Research findings are often reported opaquely, making them too difficult to decipher, interpret, and apply.
- Journalists are often cynical, even anti-intellectual, when it comes to social science research. They have not been trained in research and therefore find it easy to shun a subject they can't readily understand.
- The economics of the news business creates values among journalists that work against change. The imperative of the newsroom is to produce

enough to fill pages or air time in the least expensive way. That has led to devices such as the beat system, which in turn has led to coverage of irrelevant but easily accessible subjects—precisely what audience research would warn against.

There are many compelling reasons why journalists require knowledge of communication theories and audience behavior. First among them is the survival benefit that research-directed news work promises. In an increasingly demanding and competitive media environment, only the successful media entity offers opportunity for journalists to do their jobs. But there are other reasons:

- Journalists tend to lead cloistered lives. They associate primarily with other journalists and their sources. Therefore, audience research can help them to better know their publics. To assume that audiences can't decide what they need and want in the way of information is arrogant and elitist.
- Communication research can help journalists to write and produce stories that are more likely to be used by consumers, stories in which audience self-interest is not obscured. Research by itself is neutral. It need not lead to manipulative or cynical media practices but rather can be used to help both the public and the practitioners meet their needs.

    Where is the journalist to obtain this knowledge? There is not yet an integrated theory of communication that tells us what kinds of messages under what conditions are likely to be sought, used, and understood by people. We have only bits and pieces of theory. Still, there is much that the journalist can apply even at this stage of theoretical infancy. Some sources:
    - Books such as *Using Mass Communication Theory* by Maxwell Mc-Combs and Lee Becker (Englewood Cliffs, N.J.: Prentice-Hall, 1979), an excellent summary designed explicitly for practitioners, and *The Newspaper Survival Book, An Editor's Guide to Marketing Research,* by Philip Meyer (Bloomington, Indiana: Indiana University Press, 1985).
    - The dozens of studies sponsored by the Newspaper Readership Project, funded by a consortium of professional organizations and directed by the Newspaper Advertising Bureau.
    - Seven volumes of journalism-related research published over the years by the American Newspaper Publishers Association (ANPA) News Research Center, plus subsequent bulletins.
    - Proprietary research available at many news organizations.
    - The scholarly literature of communication, ranging through the social sciences. (This, of course, requires competent interpretation in order to be of use to journalists.)

Assessing the qualifications that contemporary journalists should possess, McCombs and Becker conclude that they need to be able to gather information and interpret events, to write well and to be sensitive to their audiences and to the social environment in which they operate. They also suggest that these characteristics of the competent journalist need something to hold them together; that glue is communication theory. Recognizing the absence of such an integrative theory, McCombs and Becker (on page 132) offer instead a set of objectives:

> Theories of communication would spell out all the relevant factors that influence human or institutional behavior, tell how all the factors are interrelated, and explain why those relationships hold. In other words, theories would tell journalists what to expect in the future. Theory would identify which messages are most likely to be received, and explain why.
>
> They would tell what kind of newsrooms are best for sound journalistic practice, and why. And they would tell publishers and general managers just what to expect the next time the federal government attempts—if it ever does again—to halt prior publication of a story. That's what good theory would do.

If there is a lack of integration of theory with practice in the news room, it is likely also to be absent in the classroom. Most newspaper recruits today (80 percent) hold degrees from journalism schools. There they are likely to have been exposed to communication theory and research but not often in newswriting and reporting classrooms. The internalization of research-related journalistic practice therefore becomes more difficult. A starting place for improvement would be the integration of theory and research throughout the curricula of schools of journalism and communication. For example, reporting classes would include information about audience motivations and characteristics as well as instruction on interviewing techniques. Courses in editorial and column writing would review the cognitive balance theories as well as library research. Editing classes would make use of uses-and-gratifications concepts as well as the stylebook.

These observations suggest a multidimensional blueprint for the academic and media worlds if research is to take its necessary place in the communication firmament. The elements of such a blueprint would include:

- An emphasis on theory-building research in the academic disciplines concerned with communication: psychology, sociology, and journalism/communication.

- Support for such basic research in the form of outright grants from the media industries. This may also come in the form of contracts for applied research, with industry sponsors making allowance for the additional work and time academic researchers will need to serve both applied and theoretical goals.
- Continued efforts by media industries to generate and sponsor applied generic research, such as that produced by the Newspaper Readership Project.
- Greater efforts by news organizations to expose their personnel to research findings and the translation of those findings into work practices. These efforts can take the form of mid-career training via in-house workshops, trade association conferences, and university-based seminars, as well as exposure to practice-oriented books and training materials.
- Integration of theory and research into journalism textbooks and classrooms at all levels.

The Practitioners Are Interested ...

But They Are Not Journalists

Sharon Dunwoody

Much of the research I do is designed to illuminate the process by which scientific and technical information finds its way into the mass media and, subsequently, into the public domain. To that end, I spend a lot of time questioning, watching, and otherwise analyzing the behaviors of the major actors in the dissemination process: sources (scientists and public information personnel) and reporters. And I make a concerted effort to offer these actors access to my findings through such devices as workshops, speeches, articles in professional newsletters, and plenty of one-on-one conversations.

Like many mass communication researchers, I have found journalists to be generally unresponsive to my work. I either bore them to tears or offend them mightily with my information. On rare occasions a science writer has asked for a copy of a research report, and rarer still are the reporters who actively solicit my advice or who endorse my activities.

But the point of this brief article is that other actors in the process *are* interested, deeply interested. And while that realization is a joyous one to those of us who devote our lives to these topics and yearn for outsiders to regard them as comparably important, it should also make us ask why some individuals regard our research as crucial while others deem our work trivial.

In my science communication domain, I find scientists and public information personnel to be far more interested in my research than are journalists. When giving a workshop to, say, mathematics professors, I always enter the room with trepidation. I fear outright rejection or, even worse, that kind of cold indifference that signals a tremendous status differential: those guys at the top and me at the bottom. But it never happens. Instead, I am met with rapt attention. No one falls asleep. No one even blinks. Everyone peppers me with questions at the end; they ask for citations to articles and books, for anything that would help them understand the process I have been discussing.

What's so different here? Why should geologists get a bigger kick out of this stuff than journalists? Why should a hospital public relations staff member find my research more functional than the medical writer at the local newspaper? Here are a few of my own speculative responses.

Maybe it's the case that in order to get excited about research you must first know enough about research to buy into the assumption that empiricism can tell you something useful. Scientists, by training, understand the value of asking and answering questions *scientifically*. They may intuitively place more faith in information placed in a peer-reviewed journal—even if they know nothing about the journal itself—because they understand that work that has negotiated peer review has been deemed good, utilitarian science by someone. Such an argument might also hold for public information personnel who, although not trained as scientists, must live with scientists and thus may have bought into many of the beliefs of the scientific culture, the value of research findings among them.

Another possible explanation is that journalists take a "ho-hum" attitude toward my work because they already know what I am about to tell them. Scientists, on the other hand, are quite ignorant of public dissemination processes and thus find my information new and of compelling interest. Indeed, some studies suggest that journalists know far more about their sources than their sources know about them. So maybe it's a simple case of catch-up.

But it is my guess that a third explanation is the most accurate one. It goes something like this: Knowledge is positively related to control. In a situation involving a variety of actors and power differentials, those who rank lower on the power scale will actively seek knowledge in order to improve their rankings.

Scientists are accorded higher status in our society than are journalists. But when a journalist actively solicits information from a scientist, that differential is reversed. It is the journalist who holds the cards (if she is good at what she does), and it is the scientist who suddenly finds herself in a subordinate position. The public information person, who often plays a critical agenda-setting role in the public dissemination of science, is often physically absent from these transactions; the result is that those individuals are often accorded no status whatsoever in the process by the other actors. The denouement of all this is that journalists are perceived by all concerned as having the most power within science communication transactions, and the sources, including public information persons, are perceived as being relatively powerless.

It is no coincidence, I would argue, that the levels of receptivity to mass communication research findings parallel this power hierarchy.

Now, this is neither good nor bad. We all jockey for power, and information gain is one generally reliable way of increasing our control over situations. If need for control is driving receptivity to information about the mass communication dissemination process, in fact, then we can improve access of journalists to research information by convincing them that such information can improve their own power positions. Let me give one example of this.

At a large scientific meeting some years back I studied the way science writers selected information for stories. Normally, findings from such a study would produce yawns at best among the journalists. But when discussing the study with them, I cast its findings in power terms. In brief, the study indicated that the scientific organization that conducted the meeting could control what became news about its own event by, among other strategies, organizing press conferences at times convenient to journalistic deadlines. Journalists, in short, did not have as much control over news decisions at that meeting as they had previously assumed.

Many of the science writers I studied disputed the findings. A few agreed with the findings. But most telling to me is the feedback I have received from the individual who conducts public information activities for this scientific organization. She argues that, since I discussed my research with the science writers, many of those journalists have largely abandoned the press conferences and are now spending more of their time at the meeting itself.

Transmitting the Data to the Professional
A Canadian Experience

PETER DESBARATS

The Canadian Journalism Database, potentially a valuable instrument for the transmission of research information to working journalists and other media professionals, emerged in 1986 from an earlier program of videotex research and development at the University of Western Ontario's Graduate School of Journalism.

The database now has five sections available to Canadian and American journalists through QL Systems, a commercial database operator in Kingston, Ontario.

The first section to go on-line was the Index to Journalism Periodicals. It was followed by Press Council Rulings, Professional Directory of Journalists, Research Papers and Reports of Proceedings, and a small database of major news items on Canadian and international media.

The graduate school's interest in computerized information systems coincided with my own arrival as dean in 1981 after a year as senior consultant and associate research director of the Royal Commission on Newspapers. In the preparation of a report for the commission on the impact of computers and new information technology on Canadian newspapers, I had talked with videotex experts and inspected videotex systems in Canada, the United States, the United Kingdom, France, and West Germany. I carried this interest into the graduate school in London, Ontario, where it caught the attention of Professor Henry Overduin, another recent arrival at the university from the ranks of working journalists.

At that time, the Canadian government was in the early throes of enthusiasm for Telidon, a high-definition system then called the "Cadillac" of videotex. "Edsel" might have been a more apt name. While the government invested large sums in the development of Telidon, under the impression that this would lead to the creation of a unique product with industrial and export possibilities, the basic principles of the system were soon incorporated in higher standards and improved systems developed in the United States and other countries. It was evident that Canada simply did not have the resources to translate its technical breakthrough into a commercial product quickly enough to outdistance its competitors, particularly in a new field as uncertain and volatile as videotex.

A positive result of this misguided enthusiasm was the rapid development of videotex expertise in Canadian corporations, laboratories, and universities. The Graduate School of Journalism at the University of Western Ontario was among the many recipients of grants from the Department of Communications in Ottawa. In our case the money was used primarily to launch Canada's first videotex news service.

In its heyday, from 1982 to 1985, Westex News supplied a full international, national, and regional news service to an agricultural database in Winnipeg, serving several thousand farmers in the provinces of Manitoba and Saskatchewan. News, primarily from The Canadian Press national news service under a shared royalty agreement, was processed by three journalists working on terminals in a small news room at the school. New material was transmitted daily from the school to Infomart, the database operator in Toronto, where it was adapted to the Telidon format and forwarded to the Winnipeg database.

Research into the usage of Westex News by prairie farmers, and its impact on previous habits of news consumption, was eventually provided to the Department of Communications in a report by Overduin. In 1984, the graduate school also hosted a Toronto conference that it advertised as the first international gathering of working videotex journalists, with participants from Canada, the United States, and Europe.

As Telidon fever abated in Ottawa and the grants dried up—the Telidon division of the Department of Communications officially ceased to exist in 1986—the school began to search for other ways to utilize its experience and expertise.

During the Westex years, the school had briefly investigated the possibility of establishing a campus videotex system at the University of Western Ontario, using the university's computer facilities. This project failed to materialize but it did start to shift the attention of Overduin and myself from large videotex systems to smaller databases for clearly defined groups of users. Our own "natural" group, of course, was Canada's journalistic community.

Partly because of its work in videotex, the school received a grant of $500,000 from the federal government in 1984 to create a new Centre for Mass Media Studies with a commitment from the University of Western Ontario to match this money within three years.

Overduin, as acting director of the centre, was conscious of the need to develop an initial project that would be useful academically but that also would persuade journalists and academics that the new centre could be a service organization. The Canadian Journalism Database seemed to be a project within the mandate and financial resources of the centre, with the promise of future growth and even revenue-producing capability down the road.

Under the direction of Kathryn Hazel, senior database editor, the Index to Journalism Periodicals became the "charter" section of the Canadian Journalism Database, input from material already assembled on paper by the school's librarian, Elizabeth Howes. It now contains more than six thousand citations of articles from academic, trade, and professional journals related to journalism and mass communication. The index is updated bimonthly by Howes, growing by more than one thousand titles a year.

The Press Council Rulings of the Canadian Journalism Database (CJD) now contain full-text decisions of all rulings by the Press Councils of Ontario and British Columbia, and Quebec Press Council rulings (in English) dating back to 1985. Permission is being sought to include rulings of the British Press Council.

As Hazel has stated, "As it now exists, this database is the electronic storehouse of current journalistic value judgments and a rich source of potential research."

Research Papers and Reports of Proceedings now contains all papers presented at the 1984 and 1985 "Encounter" conferences—annual gatherings of journalists from Canada and the Third World convened by the graduate school to discuss media and development issues. Presentations by the Quebec Press Council to the federal government and other regulatory bodies on issues of concern to Canadian media also are part of this section.

More than four hundred Canadian journalists have submitted biographical and professional information to the Professional Directory of Journalists—already a unique record of Canadian journalism professionals. Such leading Canadian journalists as Norman Webster, editor of Toronto's *Globe and Mail*, and Robert Fulford, editor of *Saturday Night* magazine, have been among the first to include themselves in this section of the database.

The media news database is in the early stages of development. Future plans include a job bank section and another containing legal rulings affecting Canadian news media.

Hazel currently is investigating a request from the ombudsman of the *Gazette* in Montreal to explore the possibility of using the Canadian Journalism Database to collect and archive the columns of ombudsmen on Canadian and U.S. newspapers.

"All these sections of the database," according to Hazel, "provide a one-of-a-kind source of material on Canadian journalism, readily accessible to anyone with a home computer and a modem."

Contributors/Participants

Louis D. Boccardi is president and general manager of the Associated Press, the world's largest news service. More than 10,000 newspapers and broadcast stations in 115 countries receive AP news and photos daily. Boccardi has become a leading spokesman on problems of readership and credibility and on First Amendment legal issues. He also has been active in the American Newspaper Publishers Association (ANPA) and the Newspaper Advertising Bureau (NAB) research oversight. A graduate of Fordham and Columbia's Graduate School of Journalism, he moved from reporter at the New York *World-Telegram & Sun* to assistant managing editor, and he held that post at the New York *World Journal Tribune*. He joined the AP in 1967 when the *WJT* ceased publication and moved through the executive ranks in steady progression.

Leo Bogart is executive president and general manager of the Newspaper Advertising Bureau (NAB). He has been president of the American Association of Opinion Research, the Radio and Television Research Council, the World Association for Public Opinion Research, the Market Research Council, and the Consumer Psychology Division of the American Psychological Association. Author of several books—including *Press and Public* (Hillsdale, N.J.: Lawrence Erlbaum, 1981)—and more than 80 articles, Bogart has received the American Association of Public Opinion Research award for distinguished contributions to public opinion research, the first Market Research Council award, and the Sidney Goldish Award for significant contributions to newspaper research. His doctorate was in sociology (University of Chicago). He has taught at several universities.

Donald J. Brenner is a professor of journalism and director of the Stephenson Research Center in the School of Journalism at the University of Missouri at Columbia. He has been a faculty member at Bowling Green State University, Northern Illinois University, and the Texas Tech University School of Medicine, where he was chairman of the Department of Health Communication. His teaching interests are in health communication, information theory, public opinion, and attitude change, and the diffu-

179

sion of innovations. His B.S. is from Bowling Green State University, his M.S. from Ohio University, and his Ph.D. from the University of Missouri at Columbia.

STEVEN H. CHAFFEE (Ph.D., Stanford University, 1965) is Janet M. Peck Professor of International Communication and chair of the Department of Communication at Stanford University. He was formerly director of the School of Journalism and Mass Communication at the University of Wisconsin-Madison. He is a past president and fellow of the International Communication Association. His research has included such topics as family interaction, political communication, adolescent socialization, interpersonal coorientation, health and prevention campaigns, and survey research methods. His publications include *Political Communication* (Beverly Hills, Calif.: Sage Publications, 1975); *Television and Human Behavior* (New York: Columbia University Press, 1978), which he wrote with George Comstock and others; and *Handbook of Communication Science* (Beverly Hills, Calif.: Sage Publications, 1987), which he wrote with Charles Berger.

BENJAMIN M. COMPAINE is a partner in Samara Associates, a strategic planning, consulting, and research group that focuses on the information industry. From 1979 to 1986 he was executive director of the Program on Information Resources Policy (PIRP) at Harvard University. Among his half dozen books are *Issues of New Information Technology* (Norwood, N.J.: Ablex Publishing, 1988), *Understanding New Media* (Cambridge, Mass.: Ballinger, 1984), and *Who Owns the Media?* (White Plains, N.Y.: Knowledge Industry Publications, 1982). His recent monographs include "Management Information: Back to Basics," "New Literacy Indicators," and "Information Technology and Cultural Change: Toward a New Literacy?"—all of which are available from PIRP. Compaine has an honors degree in political science from Dickinson College, an M.B.A. from Harvard University, and a Ph.D. from Temple University.

GEORGE COMSTOCK was director of Stanford–Peace Corps instructional television research in Bogota, Colombia, science adviser and senior research coordinator to the Surgeon General's Scientific Advisory Committee on Television and Social Behavior, and senior social psychologist at The Rand Corporation, Santa Monica, Calif., before joining Syracuse University, where he is S. I. Newhouse Professor of Public Communications. He is senior editor of the five volumes published by the National Institute of Mental Health reporting on the research commissioned for the Surgeon General's Committee, senior author of the three-volume *Television and Human Behavior* reference series (Santa Monica, Calif.: Rand, 1975), senior author of *Television and Human Behavior* (New York: Columbia University Press, 1978), author of *Television in America* (Newbury Park, Calif.: Sage Publications, 1980), and editor of *Public Communication and Behavior* (New York: Academic Press, 1986). He has written and lectured extensively on the influence of the mass media, with emphasis on the synthesis of evidence from a diversity of studies and areas of inquiry.

EDWARD R. CONY is associate editor of the *Wall Street Journal.* In 1961 he won a Pulitzer Prize for national affairs reporting. A past president of the Associated Press Managing Editors (APME), he also is vice president of the American Society of Newspaper Editors (ASNE). Born in Maine, Cony attended Colby College, served in the Army from 1943 to 1946, graduated with a B.A. in political science from Reed College in 1948, and added a journalism M.A. in 1951 at Stanford. After reporting for the Portland *Oregonian*, he joined the *Wall Street Journal*.

MELVIN L. DE FLEUR received his B.S. degree in psychology at St. Louis University and the M.A. and Ph.D. in sociology at the University of Washington. He has been on the faculty at several universities, including Indiana, Kentucky, Washington State, New Mexico, and Miami. Currently he occupies the John Ben Snow Endowed Chair in the Newhouse School at Syracuse University. He has published numerous articles on various aspects of mass communication. His books include *The Flow of Information* (East Brunswick, N.J.: Transaction Books, 1986); *Theories of Mass Communication* (White Plains, N.Y.: Longman, 1981); *Understanding Mass Communication* (Boston: Houghton Mifflin, 1981); *Milestones in Mass Communication Research* (White Plains, N.Y.: Longman, 1983), and a number of others.

EVERETTE E. DENNIS is the executive director of the Gannett Center for Media Studies at Columbia University, the nation's first institute for the advanced study of mass communication and technological change. Before joining the Gannett Foundation, Dennis was dean of the School of Journalism at the University of Oregon. While at Oregon he also headed the Project on the Future of Journalism Education and served as national president of the Association for Education in Journalism and Mass Communication (AEJMC). He also has taught at Northwestern, Minnesota, and Kansas State. Author, coauthor, and editor of more than a dozen books, Dennis has written and lectured widely about media and society issues, communication law, and other topics. His books include the popular text, *Understanding Mass Communication*, coauthored with Melvin L. De Fleur (Boston: Houghton Mifflin, 1981), *The Media Society* (New York: Macmillan, 1983), and *Justice Hugo Black and the First Amendment* (Ames, Iowa: Iowa State University Press, 1978). He has also written more than sixty magazine and journal articles. His honors include several fellowship appointments. Dennis took his B.S. at Oregon, his M.A. at Syracuse, and his Ph.D. at Minnesota.

PETER DESBARATS has been dean of the Graduate School of Journalism at the University of Western Ontario in London, Ontario, Canada, since 1981. In 1980–81 he was senior consultant and associate research director of the Royal Commission on Newspapers. Before that he worked for thirty years as a print and electronic journalist for Canadian newspapers, magazines, and television networks. He is the founding president of the Association of Directors of Journalism Programs in Canadian Universities and is currently working on a guide to Canadian news media to be published by Harcourt Brace.

SHARON DUNWOODY is associate professor of journalism and mass communication and also heads the Center for Environmental Communications and Education Studies at the University of Wisconsin–Madison. A former newspaper science writer, Professor Dunwoody earned her undergraduate degree in journalism at Indiana University, a master's in mass communication from Temple University, and a Ph.D. in mass communication from Indiana University. She taught journalism at Ohio State University before going to the University of Wisconsin in 1981. She does research on issues bearing on the public understanding of science, particularly those concerned with media coverage of science and technology.

ALEX S. EDELSTEIN, a member of the faculty of the University of Washington since 1966 and director of its School of Communications from 1973 to 1981, is a graduate of San Francisco State University (B.A.), Stanford University (M.A.), and the University of Minnesota (Ph.D.). Edelstein has done media research on the role of the newspaper in the community, leadership role of editors, readership and reader interest, analysis of news, media credibility, and audience characteristics relating to credibility. He has carried out a great deal of this research in an international and comparative setting in Finland, Germany, Denmark, Japan, Hong Kong, Malaysia, and Yugoslavia. He is the author of *Comparative Communication Research* (Beverly Hills, Calif.: Sage Publications, 1982), *The Uses of Communication in Decision-Making* (New York: Praeger, 1974), *Information Societies: Comparing the Japanese and American Experiences* (Seattle, Wash.: International Communication Center, 1978), and *Perspectives in Mass Communication* (Copenhagen: Einar Harck, 1966). A former and still occasional journalist, he is now completing a book entitled *International Communication and Comparative Behavior*.

OSCAR H. GANDY, JR., is associate professor of communications at the Annenberg School of Communications at the University of Pennsylvania. Formerly, he was the director of the Center for Communications Research at Howard University, where he taught for ten years. He received his doctorate in public affairs communication from Stanford University. His writing and research has concentrated primarily on the political economy of communication and information. He is the author of *Beyond Agenda Setting: Information Subsidies and Public Policy* (Norwood, N.J.: Ablex Publishers, 1982), was a founding member of the Union for Democratic Communications, and has served as the chairman of the organizing committee for the Annual Telecommunications Policy Research Conference.

GEORGE GERBNER is dean of the Annenberg School of Communications at the University of Pennsylvania. He has a long record of U.S. and multinational mass communications projects, has written extensively, and is executive editor of the quarterly *Journal of Communication*. Born in Hungary, he came to the United States in 1939, received his B.A. at the University of California–Berkeley, and his M.S. and Ph.D. at the University of Southern California. He has taught at the University of Illinois' Institute of Communications Research and El Camino and John Muir colleges. He served on the staff of the San Francisco *Chronicle* and was a member of the Office of Strategic Services in World War II. Gerbner was editor of the widely-discussed 1983 special issue of the *Journal of Communication*, "Ferment in the Field," which covered many critical research issues.

ALBERT E. GOLLIN is vice president and associate research director at the Newspaper Advertising Bureau (NAB), New York City. Trained as a sociologist at Columbia University, where he earned a Ph.D. under Paul F. Lazarsfeld and Herbert H. Hyman, he has specialized in the conduct of applied social research throughout his career. He joined NAB in 1977 after having worked at Columbia's Bureau of Applied Social Research and at the Bureau of Social Science Research, Washington, D.C.—both pioneering centers of communications and social research. He has been elected president of the District of Columbia Sociological Society, chairman of the Sociological Practice Section, American Sociological Association, and president of the American Association for Public Opinion Research. He has published widely in sociological and communications journals and was the inaugural recipient in 1983 of the Zarwell Award for newspaper research by the Newspaper Research Council.

MARGARET T. GORDON is director of the Center for Urban Affairs and Policy Research at Northwestern University and a professor of journalism, sociology, and urban affairs. She is also director of research at the Medill School of Journalism. Her own research is currently focusing on the effects of mass media on the policy-making process. She is directing a project on the impact of investigative journalism on the public, interest group leaders, and policy. While she was a senior fellow at the Gannett Center for Media Studies at Columbia University in 1985, Professor Gordon began research on the relationships between the press and institutions they cover. She holds three degrees from Northwestern, including a Ph.D. in sociology. She serves on the National Academy of Sciences Committee on National Urban Policy and several other national and local committees and commissions.

JUDITH D. HINES is vice president and director of the American Newspaper Publishers Association (ANPA) Foundation, overseeing projects aimed at better journalism education, stronger public support for a free press, and development of informed and intelligent newspaper readers. She served for five years as manager of educational services before becoming director of the ANPA Foundation in 1979. She received her B.A. in English from Duke University and has done graduate work at the University of Virginia. She taught for a brief period and has tutored at all grade levels. She has edited newsletters, assisted the director of a U.S. Office of Education teacher-training program, and worked on a management-improvement program for public housing.

NORMAN E. ISAACS is a consultant, writer, and lecturer. British-born, he came to the United States as a teenager and entered journalism at seventeen as a sports cub. In ten years he was managing editor and went on to edit five prize-winning metropolitan papers, turn educator, and be associate dean at Columbia's Graduate School. Later he returned to being a publisher, was a visiting professor at Stanford, and directed the Jefferson Fellowships at the East-West Center in Hawaii. Recipient of many awards from both print and broadcast groups, he has been president of both the Associated Press Managing Editors (APME) and the American Society of Newspaper Editors (ASNE) and is regarded as one of the leading spokesmen on journalistic ethics. The author of *Untended Gates: The Mismanaged Press* (New York: Columbia University Press, 1986), Isaacs was awarded an honorary doctor of letters degree (D. Litt.) in 1987 by Syracuse University.

ARNOLD H. ISMACH is dean of the School of Journalism at the University of Oregon, where he came after twelve years on the faculty of the School of Journalism and Mass Communication at the University of Minnesota. A native of New York City, he holds degrees from the University of Oklahoma (B.A.), University of California at Los Angeles (M.A.), and the University of Washington (Ph.D.). He worked as a newspaper reporter and editor in Washington and California for fifteen years before turning to journalism education. The coauthor of three journalism textbooks, he is a frequent consultant to news organizations and has worked for almost twenty years as a political campaign consultant. A specialist on public opinion measurement, he has written extensively on polls and surveys.

MARK R. LEVY is a professor in the College of Journalism and a research associate of the Center for Research in Public Communication at the University of Maryland. His principal research interests are uses and gratifications theory, news comprehension, and the impact of new communication technologies on audience behavior. Before earning his Ph.D. from Columbia University, he was a newspaper reporter, writer, editor, and associate producer with NBC in New York, and an associate national affairs editor at *Newsweek*. He has been a consultant to the National Association of Broadcasters, the Motion Picture Association of America, NBC News, and the Independent Broadcasting Authority in London.

KRISTIN MCGRATH, president of Minnesota Opinion Research Inc. (MORI), has worked in research and journalism for nearly twenty years including six years as research director for the Minneapolis *Star Tribune*. In that capacity she supervised the Minnesota Poll, a continuous statewide survey of opinion. It was her company that carried out the 1985 newspaper credibility studies for the American Society of Newspaper Editors ("Newspaper Credibility: Building Reader Trust") and the Associated Press Managing Editors ("Journalists and Readers: Bridging the Credibility Gap"). Prior to her involvement in research she was an award-winning reporter and an assistant news editor. McGrath has a B.A. from Carleton College, an M.A. from Stanford University, and a Ph.D. from the University of Minnesota. She has served as vice president of both the Newspaper Research Council and the Minnesota Chapter of the American Marketing Association and has taught journalism and research at Northwestern University's Medill School of Journalism and the University of Minnesota. McGrath also spent a year in India as a Fulbright Fellow and a year in Paris as a student at the Sorbonne.

PHILIP MEYER is the William Rand Kenan, Jr., Professor of Journalism at the University of North Carolina at Chapel Hill. Former director of news and circulation research for the Knight-Ridder Newspapers, he has also worked as a reporter for the *Miami Herald* and a national correspondent for Knight-Ridder Newspapers. A Nieman Fellow at Harvard University in 1966, he spent the summer of 1985 as a senior fellow at the Gannett Center for Media Studies. His bachelor's degree in technical journalism is from Kansas State University and his master's in political science is from the University of North Carolina. He has served on the editorial boards of *Public Opinion Quarterly* and the *Newspaper Research Journal*. His most recent book is *Ethical Journalism* (White Plains, N.Y.: Longman, 1987).

L. EDWARD MULLINS is dean of the School of Communication at the University of Alabama. Previously, he was associate dean of the school and director of its Research Center. He has a master's in journalism from Ohio State University and a Ph.D. in mass communication from the University of North Carolina at Chapel Hill. Mullins is a former newspaper reporter, copy editor, and news executive, with experience on newspapers in Georgia, Texas, Ohio, and North Carolina. He has served as a news room consultant for a number of daily newspapers and public relations operations. He is a member of the editorial board of Newspaper Research Journal. He co-founded the Capstone Poll, a leading academic poll, at the University of Alabama.

J. LEONARD REINSCH is chairman of Sunbelt Cable (Fla.) and the former chairman of Cox Broadcasting Corp. Reinsch became widely known for his work in political broadcast journalism, which began in 1944. He was an adviser to presidents Franklin Delano Roosevelt and Harry S Truman and for the 1952 Democratic National Convention, the first to go on network television coast to coast. He helped arrange the first Presidential debates and was TV director of the 1960 Kennedy-Nixon debates. Reinsch is a member of the Carnegie Commission on the Future of Broadcasting. He has received the International Radio and Television Society's Gold Medal Award, the National Association of Broadcasters' Distinguished Service Award, and the Keller Award from his alma mater, Northwestern University.

JOHN P. ROBINSON is professor of sociology and director of the Survey Research Center at the University of Maryland. He is the author of *How Americans Use Time* (New York: Praeger, 1977) and coauthor of *The Main Source: Learning From Television News* (Beverly Hills, Calif.: Sage Publications, 1986), *Polls Apart* (Cabin John, Md.: Seven Looks Press, 1982), and *Measures of Social Psychological Attitudes* (Ann Arbor, Mich.: Survey Research Center, Institute for Social Research, 1969, 1973). He was research coordinator for the U.S. Surgeon General's study on communication and human behavior and research adviser to BBC News. His research interests include the public's use of time, mass media audiences, new communication technologies, arts participation, and social science methodology.

DAVID M. RUBIN is codirector of the Center for War, Peace, and the News Media at New York University, a research and teaching center that studies press coverage of the arms race and United States–Soviet relations. He is professor and former chair of the Department of Journalism and Mass Communication at NYU. He is on the board of directors of the Committee to Protect Journalists and is chair of the Communications Media Committee of the American Civil Liberties Union. He has written widely about the mass media, with particular attention to First Amendment issues, journalism ethics, and the press and national security. His B.A. is from Columbia University, and his M.A. and Ph.D. are from Stanford University.

KEITH P. SANDERS is a professor at the School of Journalism at the University of Missouri–Columbia. An associate editor of *Mass Comm Review*, he served on the editorial board of *Journalism Monographs* for several years. He was the 1987 recipient of the Trayes' Professor of the Year award presented by the Mass Communication & Society Division of the Association for Education in Journalism and Mass Communication (AEJMC). He has been Editorial Department chairman and associate dean at Missouri. His major research interests are mass-media effects, audience analysis, and political campaign strategies. His B.S. is from Bowling Green State University, his M.A. is from Ohio University, and his Ph.D. is from the University of Iowa.

NANCY WEATHERLY SHARP is an associate professor in the Newspaper Department of Syracuse University's S. I. Newhouse School of Public Communications. A graduate of the University of Missouri (B.J.) and Syracuse University (M.S.Sc.), she is a former staff writer for the Columbia, Mo., *Daily Tribune*; the State of Missouri Historical Society's *Missouri Historical Review*; the Hayward, Calif., *Daily Review*; the Oakland, Calif., *Tribune*; and the Syracuse, N.Y., *Herald-Journal*. She is first author of *Faculty Women in Journalism and Mass Communications: Problems and Progress* (Syracuse, N.Y., 1985), and editor of *The Corporation in a Changing Society* and *Informing America: Who Is Responsible for What?* (proceedings, respectively, of the 1982 and 1983 MacNaughton symposiums in New York). Professor Sharp is working as coauthor of a book, *American Legislative Leaders, 1911–1982*, under contract with Greenwood Press. She serves on the editorial board of the *Newspaper Research Journal*.

FRANK STANTON is president emeritus of CBS Inc. and chairman emeritus of the American Red Cross. After receiving his Ph.D. at Ohio State University in 1935, he joined CBS's research department and rose to be president from 1946 through 1971. He was chairman of the U.S. Advisory Commission on Information for nine years, chairman of the Rand Corp., founding chair of the Center for Advanced Study in the Behavioral Sciences, and chair of the Carnegie Institution of Washington. Awards have been showered on him, several for his strong defense of broadcast journalists' Constitutional rights. Harvard and Cooper Union both have Frank Stanton professorial chairs, and the Red Cross maintains the Frank Stanton Production Center in Falls Church, Va. He is active on more than a dozen major commissions and boards.

GUIDO H. STEMPEL III is distinguished professor of journalism at the E. W. Scripps School of Journalism at Ohio University, where he has taught since 1965. He was director of that school from 1972 to 1979 and again in 1985–86. He has been editor of *Journalism Quarterly* since 1972 and was associate editor of that journal from 1970 to 1972. He is coauthor and coeditor of *Research Methods in Mass Communication* (Englewood Cliffs, N.J.: Prentice-Hall, 1981), the most widely-used text in that field. He is a regular contributor to *presstime* and the author of more than one hundred journal and magazine articles, including twenty-two in *Journalism Quarterly*. He received the Chancellor's Award for Distinguished Service to the Field of Journalism from the University of Wisconsin in 1977. His bachelor's and master's degrees in journalism are from Indiana University and his Ph.D. from the University of Wisconsin.

EDWARD C. STEPHENS is dean of the S.I. Newhouse School of Public Communications and came to Syracuse University in 1976 as chairman of the Department of Advertising. A former professor at Northwestern University, he had worked for ten years as a creative supervisor and account executive at Dancer Fitzgerald Sample in New York City. Dean Stephens is an active consultant to advertising agencies in the creation of educational programs and development of executive talent. His bachelor's degree is from Occidental College and his master's from the Medill School of Journalism at Northwestern University.

JOHN D. STEVENS is professor and former chair of communication at the University of Michigan. He received his Ph.D. from the University of Wisconsin. He has served as head of the Association for Education in Journalism and Mass Communication (AEJMC) History Division and has published extensively on mass-media history and First Amendment questions. His books are *Mass Media Between the Wars: Perceptions of Cultural Tension, 1918–41* (Syracuse, N.Y.: Syracuse University Press, 1984), which he wrote with Catherine L. Covert; *Shaping the First Amendment: The Development of Free Expression* (Newbury Park, Calif.: Sage Publications, 1982); *Communication History* (Newbury Park, Calif.: Sage Publications, 1980), with Hazel D. Garcia; *The Rest of the Elephant: Perspectives on the Mass Media* (New York: Prentice-Hall, 1973), with William Porter; *Mass Media and the National Experience* (New York: Harper & Row, 1971), with Ronald T. Farrar.

GERALD STONE is professor and coordinator of graduate studies at Memphis State University and editor of the *Newspaper Research Journal*, a quarterly journal of practical research for the newspaper industry. Stone has worked in public relations and news, having been a daily newspaper wire deskman, a bureau correspondent with Associated Press, editor of a weekly newspaper, and managing editor of a monthly magazine. He teaches news and feature writing, research methods, and mass communication theories at Memphis State Univeristy, where he previously was chairman of the journalism department. His Ph.D. in mass communications is from Syracuse University.

ALEXIS TAN (Ph.D., University of Wisconsin) is professor and chair of the Department of Communications, Washington State University. He is the author of *Mass Communication Theories and Research* (New York: Macmillan, 2nd ed. 1985) and of more than forty book chapters and research articles in *Journalism Quarterly, Journal of Communication, Public Opinion Quarterly, Journal of Broadcasting, The Quarterly Journal of Speech* and *Communication Monographs*. He has taught at the University of the Philippines, Cornell University, and Texas Tech University. He is a student of Eastern religions and the martial arts. He is working on a book about information processing and new communications technology.

DANIEL B. WACKMAN is a professor in the School of Journalism and Mass Communication at the University of Minnesota. His teaching specialties include advertising, media management, and research methodology. For eleven years Professor Wackman was director of the Communication Research Division in the School of Journalism and Mass Communication, his research focusing on television advertising directed toward children and its impact on children's socialization as consumers. He has testified before the Federal Trade Commission in conjunction with FTC proposals to restrict advertising directed toward children. Recently his research has focused on organizational aspects of mass communication, and he has coauthored a textbook on media management entitled *Managing Media Organizations: Effective Leadership of the Media* (White Plains, N.Y.: Longman, 1987). Wackman earned his Ph.D. from the University of Wisconsin at Madison.

DAVID H. WEAVER is professor of journalism at Indiana University and director of the Bureau of Media Research in the School of Journalism. He is president of the Association for Education in Journalism and Mass Communication (AEJMC) and past president of the Midwest Association for Public Opinion Research (MAPOR). He received his Ph.D. in mass communication research from the University of North Carolina in 1974 after having worked as an editor and reporter on daily newspapers in Indiana and North Carolina. He is the recipient of the third annual AEJMC/Krieghbaum Under-40 Award to recognize and encourage excellence in teaching, research, and service in journalism and mass communication. He is the author of *Videotex Journalism* (Hillsdale, N.J.: Erlbaum, 1983), senior author of *Media Agenda-Setting in a Presidential Election* (New York: Praeger, 1981), coauthor (with G. Cleveland Wilhoit) of *Newsroom Guide to Polls and Surveys* (Washington, D.C.: American Newspaper Publishers Association, 1980), and author of numerous book chapters and articles on media agenda-setting, newspaper readership, and foreign news coverage. He is also senior author (with G. Cleveland Wilhoit) of *The American Journalist: A Portrait of U.S. News People and Their Work* (Bloomington, Ind.: Indiana University Press, 1986). Professor Weaver serves on the editorial boards of *Journalism Quarterly*, the *Newspaper Research Journal*, and the Sage *Mass Communication Review Yearbooks*.

SHIRLEY WILKINS is president of the Roper Organization and has been engaged in marketing and opinion research since 1953. She has been codirector of the biennial surveys on Public Attitudes Toward Television and directed a study on sex, profanity, and violence in TV programs for NBC. With Burns Roper, she developed *Roper Reports*, the public opinion research survey subscribed to by leading business, governmental, and nonprofit organizations. Her experience in conducting research projects has been wide and varied, and in 1977 she received the YWCA's Elizabeth Cutter Morrow Award for distinguished women in business. Born in Norfolk, Va., she is a graduate of James Madison University.

BRIAN WINSTON, now dean of the School of Communications at Pennsylvania State University, was the research director of the Glasgow University Department of Sociology News Media Research Group—which produced *Bad News* (London: Routledge and Kegan Paul, 1976) and *More Bad News* (London: Routledge and Kegan Paul, 1980). He has contributed regularly to *Channels* (New York), *The Listener, Stills,* and *Sight and Sound* (London) and was the television critic of the *Soho Weekly News* in New York. He won an Emmy award for documentary script writing in 1985 and has produced one feature film (in Canada starring William Schatner). In addition to the Glasgow Media Group's work, his books include: *Dangling Conversations: The Image of the Media* (London: Davis-Poynter, 1973), *Dangling Conversations: Hardware/Software* (London: Davis-Poynter, 1974), *Misunderstanding Media* (Cambridge, Mass.: Harvard University Press, 1986), and *Working With Video* (New York: Amphoto, 1986).

FREDERICK T. C. YU is the CBS Professor of International Journalism and acting dean at Columbia University's Graduate School of Journalism. Widely known in media research, he is author and coauthor of a number of books. His undergraduate work was done at the University of Nanking in China. He received his M.A. and Ph.D. at the University of Iowa, and he was a Ford Foundation post-doctoral fellow at Harvard University and Massachusetts Institute of Technology. Prior to joining Columbia, Dr. Yu was on the editorial staffs of the *Springfield News-Sun* (Ohio) and the *Washington Post*. His chief research colleague has been Dr. W. Phillips Davison. They have collaborated on extensive studies into mass-media systems and their effects and also on major issues and future directions.

Index

COMMUNICATIONS RESEARCH

was composed in 10½ on 12 Janson on Digital Compugraphic equipment
by Metricomp;
with display type set in Martin Gothic Bold
by Dix Type Inc.;
printed by sheet-fed offset on 50-pound, acid-free Glatfelter Natural Hi-Bulk,
Smyth sewn and bound over binder's boards in Joanna Arrestox B,
and notch bound with paper covers printed in two colors
by Braun-Brumfield, Inc.;
designed by Will Underwood;
and published by

SYRACUSE UNIVERSITY PRESS
SYRACUSE, NEW YORK 13244-5160

DATE DUE

MAY 2 3 1989 MAY 3 1 RECD			